The Recruiter Guide

An Instructional Manual:

Discover Financial Independence
in the
Healthcare Recruiting Industry

The Recruiter Guide

Authors:
Angela Allen-Cornelius
Marla Little
Randy T. Little

The Recruiter Guide
First Edition

ISBN: 978-0-557-57048-5

TABLE OF CONTENTS

Section One:

Guide to Healthcare Recruitment

HEALTHCARE RECRUITMENT

With 40 years of combined experience in the field of recruitment, these three business owners, entrepreneurs, and recruiters have finally put their experience and knowledge into this comprehensive Healthcare Recruitment Guide. This book deals with the extremely lucrative and exciting field of Physician Recruitment. Not only have these three individuals trained many recruiters, but they have operated their own successful firms as well as the longest running, and most established network of healthcare recruiters. Their collaboration has produced this comprehensive guide for both the self-starter, and the experienced recruiter. Your dream occupation is condensed into this easy to understand and follow manual. Let's get the show on the road!

PHYSICIAN RECRUITMENT or HOW TO BECOME A HEADHUNTER

Welcome to the exciting vocation of Recruitment. You may have heard the term Headhunter or Agent as well. Basically, a Recruiter secures a client (employer) who will pay the Recruiter a fee (either flat fee or percentage of first year income) to find a Candidate who will fit the needs of the employer.

Sounds simple, right? Wrong…recruitment is a detail oriented "people" business which takes dedication, tenacity, honesty, and humor in order to be successful. The very positive point about becoming a Recruiter is that you can work from a home office. A new business must become established and that is what you are doing…becoming established.

Many programs that teach you how to recruit would cost upwards to $150,000. You should make an investment for your future, but that investment can be much more manageable. This manual will teach you how to Recruit; set up an office; and to live the life of which dreams are made. AND, it will do it in an affordable manner. You've made the decision…So, let's get to it!

SET YOUR GOAL

Set two figures that are alternate goals.

Figure 1: This monetary figure is the amount of money you **NEED** this year to pay your bills and have a little left over. Put that figure on one side of a small sheet of paper or an icon on your computer screen. That determines exactly how much you need to make per year. Be realistic with this figure and don't be shy.

Figure 2: This monetary figure is the amount of money you **WANT** to make this year. Do you want to build a house? Do you want to buy a new car? Do you want to put money into a child's college fund? This figure is your dream figure. Put that figure next to your Need figure.

Example Yearly Goals

Need (Expenses)			**Want**	
House Payment & Insurance	$14,500		Expenses	$31,500
Utilities	$2,400		House fund	$10,000
Household Expenses (food, gas, etc)	$6,500		New Car Payment	$8,400
Credit Card Payment	$1,200		Entertainment	$3,000
Car Insurance	$900		Retirement Plan	$3,500
Health Insurance	$2,400		Vacation/Trips	$5,000
Student Loans	$3,600		Charity	$1,000
Total	**$31,500**		**Total**	**$62,400**

Your **GOAL** is to meet your **WANT** figure. The **NEED** figure will be automatic if you shoot for your Figure 2. Later in the manual we will explain how you go about achieving the goals.

WHAT IS A RECRUITER?

This is your occupational term. As a **Recruiter** you are similar to a Personnel Consultant. A Recruiter locates a qualified candidate to fit the employer's requirements and job description.

A Recruiter **RECRUITS** a candidate and **PLACES** that candidate with the **CLIENT.**

TERMS

It is important to become familiar with these common terms and phrases related to recruiting. Most topics are covered in more depth throughout the manual.

External Recruiter: Known simply as **Recruiter** is a term used to describe the individual who contracts with an employer to find candidates. This manual teaches you to become an external Recruiter.

Internal Recruiter: Term used to describe the individual within the Employment site who works with the External Recruiter. This is the individual who is your primary contact within your Client's walls.

Client: This is the employer. This employer can be a business, hospital, clinic, etc. This client can be either profit or non profit. The client signs your contract and pays your fee. The Internal Recruiter works for this employer.

Candidate: This is your "gold". This is the individual you recruit to fill the job opening for which you have contracted with the Client.

Physician: This term applies to your candidate. The physician is either a Medical Doctor or MD meaning he or she graduated from a University Program and received a Doctorate of Medicine or he/she can be a Doctor of Osteopathy or DO meaning graduation from a school of Osteopathic Medicine.

Physician Assistant: This candidate also referred to as a PA-C has graduated from an accredited program to become a PA. He/She has a Bachelor's Degree as well as graduate study in the area. Graduate study usually entails two extra post graduate years. The Physician Assistant is a sometimes referred to as a Mid-Level Practitioner. The PA performs many of the same duties as the doctor: Taking medical histories, examining patients, ordering lab and x-ray; and in some case prescribing treatment. Each State determines the level at which the PA can perform. The American Academy of Physician Assistants will have links to each state's Department of Health requirements. Also, the Accreditation Review Commission on Education for the Physician Assistant (ARC-PA) requires that all PA training programs offer graduate level degrees. After graduation from an accredited program, the PA must pass the Physician Assistant National Certifying Exam (PANCE).

Nurse Practitioner: This candidate also referred to as an NP is a Registered Nurse (RN); has graduated from an accredited nursing program; and has obtained a Master's Degree in an accredited program for Nurse Practitioner training. A Nurse Practitioner must obtain a state license to practice and pass the NCLEX-RN (National Council

Licensing Examination-Registered Nurse) exam. The Nurse Practitioner, also sometimes referred to as a Mid-Level Practitioner, is able to examine, diagnose and treat patients. Most states allow the NP to prescribe medications as well. The NP can run an office independent of a physician, but usually has a licensed physician who reviews the patient's chart and signs off on it also.

CRNA: Certified Registered Nurse Anesthetist: This candidate is a Nurse Practitioner, but is specialized in Anesthesia. The CRNA is a Bachelor's trained RN (Registered Nurse) or other appropriately trained RN; licensed as an RN; has one year of acute care experience; and graduates from a certified CRNA training program which is a Master's Degree program. The CRNA can work independently of a physician and performs all duties of the Anesthetist.

Contract: This is the document which states your fee and conditions of the hire. It is usually signed by the recruiter and the Client representative. In some cases you provide the contract. In other cases the Client has a standard contract. Read this contract carefully. Remember, this is the document that supports your claim to a fee. A contract can be a "**Contingency**" contract which means that you are paid a fee only if you locate a candidate who is hired by the Client. A contract can be a "**Retained**" contract which means that your Client retains you as its recruiter and pays you a predetermined amount throughout the search period. Another contract can be a "**Locum Tenens**" contract which means you are providing a doctor who is a "fill-in" for the client.

Fee: This is the amount you charge the client to find a candidate who is hired by your client. Fees range from flat fees to percentages of the candidate's first year salary.

Guarantee: This is usually outlined clearly in the contract. It is what you guarantee the employer should the hired candidate not work out for the Client within a designated period of time. This is extremely important for you to review.

Database: Every recruiter should have a good internal computerized database. This can be one you create; one you buy; or one from a network to which you subscribe. Whatever form you use, you need to have a system for keeping accurate notes; putting in all documents such as CV's, contracts, emails, faxes, notes on both clients and candidates. A good database will also have an area for tickler notes and updates. You must keep a good record of all activity. You never know when you will need to prove that a placement is yours.

Placement: This is your money ticket. This is the term used when you have supplied a candidate to your client and your client hires the candidate and pays you the fee. This is also a term used when a trading partner takes your candidate and places the candidate with his/her client and pays you half of the fee.

Sourcing: This is the term that applies to both sides of the recruitment business: Job sourcing and Candidate sourcing. You will learn how to find your clients which become your job order. You will also learn how to locate your candidates so you can fill those job orders.

Placement stages: After you have a signed contract or fee agreement, you get the job order from your client and begin contacting potential candidates. You get a candidate interested in your job. You get the client interested in your candidate. A telephone interview is arranged between the client and candidate. An onsite interview is conducted between the client and candidate. The client offers the candidate the job. The candidate accepts the offer. The candidate signs the client's contract (if there is a contract). You get paid half the fee. The client starts his job. You get paid the other half of the fee.

CV vs. Resume: *CV* stands for Curriculum Vitae and it is the document provided by a Physician or other highly trained Candidate. This provides the Candidate's personal contact information; education; training; employment history; research; publications, etc. It is typically longer and more inclusive than a resume. *Resume* is the term used to describe the document for all other candidates. It, too, has all of the pertinent information concerning a candidate, but is often formatted to summarize achievements.

Visa: This is a term used to describe a Candidate's citizenship status. He/she has not had his/her degree from the United States or a United States territory and does not have a green card or is not a US citizen. This is the Candidate who has entered the US on a Visa. There are a variety of these which will be discussed later. He or she has gotten the degree from a foreign or international institution and is in the United States under a particular visa. You need to make sure your Client will look at a Visa Candidate prior to presenting the CV or Resume of a candidate on a Visa.

Job Order: This term refers to the information you receive from the Client which describes the job for which the Client has contracted your services. A job order should be detailed and include the name of the Client; job location; type of job; job details and requirements; salary; etc. Sample job order forms will be included in this manual.

Candidate Profile: This term refers to the information you glean from the Candidate during your interview with the candidate. Information on the candidate profile may or may not be on the Candidate's CV or Resume. You are getting a full profile of the candidate in order to make a good match with your client. Candidate profile forms will be included in this manual.

EEOC: This is the term which refers to the Equal Employment Opportunity Commission. There is a strict set of guidelines which lets you know what you can or cannot discriminate against. You cannot discriminate according to Age, Gender, National origin, disability, to name a few. If your Client wants you to advertise the job and wants you to say that you will only look at a certain gender, you cannot do this. You can read full EEOC requirements by doing an Internet search.

Discrimination: This term refers to the above EEOC regulations. It is illegal to discriminate according to the EEOC guidelines.

Split business: Many recruiters do "split business." This is a term which means that you are asking another recruiter to assist you with either a search for a candidate to fit your job or a search for a job to fit your candidate. Once the placement is completed, the two of you share in the fee. That is, unless you belong to an organized network of Recruiters (i.e., The Alliance of Medical Recruiters), you will need to have a "split fee agreement." Not all networks have policies to cover split business. Be sure to read their policies carefully. Split business is discussed further at the end of this section.

Split fee agreement: If you do a split fee with another recruiter, you will need to have a "Split Fee Agreement" with that other recruiter. This agreement outlines the terms of your business relationship together. If you belong to a network like The Alliance of Medical Recruiters (AMR), you do not need a Split fee agreement with other AMR members because all of you agree to the same agreement when you join the network. An example agreement is at the end of this section.

Trading Partner: This term refers to a recruiter outside of your firm with whom you are doing split business. If you have the job opportunity and are looking for a candidate from a trading partner, always remember to "Clear the Name." with your colleague. You do not want to accept a candidate you already have in your system. Remember, though, you must have had direct contact with that candidate and not just have a name. You will lose trading partners quickly if you try that type of business.

Clearing a Name: When you work with other firms on a split fee arrangement, it is a common practice to clear names. That means that if you have a job and your trading partner has a candidate, you will ask your trading partner to give you the candidate's last name so that you can make sure you do not have the candidate. Having a candidate means that you have made direct contact with the candidate via phone, email, etc. and you have or are receiving the CV or Resume. You cannot use a database, list, phone book, internet site, etc. and claim a candidate purely by name. It is always a good habit to clear a name with a trading partner because you may have taken that candidate from a different trading partner. You do not want to be in a position where you are accepting the same candidate from two trading partners.

VISA ISSUES

Many candidates will complete their medical degree in another country and come to the United States to enter a residency program. Most of the time, the candidates will be here on a visa that requires sponsorship. In order to find an appropriate placement for them, you will need to be familiar with visa issues.

US Training means that a candidate has received ALL of his/her professional training in the US or Puerto Rico which is a US held territory.

International Training means that the candidate has received his/her primary training (i.e. medical degree) outside the US. This may sometimes be referred to as Foreign Training. In the case of a physician, this refers to a physician who has received his/her medical degree in a country outside the US and US territories. Then, that physician does his/her residency training in the US. All states require a physician to have US residencies before he/she can be licensed. In the physician recruitment arena, these candidates are many times referred to as **IMG's** (International Medical Graduates) or **FMG's** (Foreign Medical Graduates)

It is necessary to distinguish between these two trainings for two primary reasons: **1. State or National licensure or certification for the candidate 2. Client acceptance of training.** You will need to make sure that your client will accept a candidate who has international or foreign training. Remember: it is not illegal to accept or ask for candidates with certain training. To understand the type of visa under which your candidate falls, it is suggested strongly that you do an internet search on an Immigration Attorney website. Below you will see categories of "Temporary Visas". Most of these visas will not pertain to your candidate. Some of the important areas are **J-1; H1-B; O** Sometimes there are exceptions, so your visa candidate must clarify his/her status with his/her immigration attorney. Immigration laws are constantly changing which is why your visa candidate must be aware of these changes.

- Visitors for Business or Pleasure ("B-1/B-2") - (CIS)
- Visitor Visas to the U.S. (State Department)
- Visa Waiver Program (State Department)
- Duration of Mexican Border Crossing Cards Extended to 30 Days
- Crewmen ("D-1")
- Treaty Traders ("E-1")
- Treaty Investors ("E-2")
- FAQ - Law Re: Employment For Spouses Of Persons In E/L Status

- INS Memorandum Re: E/L Law (February 22, 2002)
- Australian Professionals ("E-3") (U.S. Embassy, Canberra, Australia)
- E-3 Regulations (State Department) - September 2, 2005
- USCIS Guidance on E-3 classification - January 6, 2006
- Students ("F-1")
- Temporary Professional Workers ("H-1B")
- Temporary Agricultural Workers ("H-2A")
- Temporary Skilled and Unskilled Workers ("H-2B")
- Trainees ("H-3")
- Foreign Journalists ("I")
- Exchange Visitors ("J-1")
- Fiancées of U.S. Citizens ("K-1")
- Spouses of U.S. Citizens ("K-3")
- Intracompany Transferees ("L-1")
- Vocational Students ("M-1")
- Persons of Extraordinary Ability ("O")
- Regulations: Petitioning Requirements for the O and P Nonimmigrant Classifications (4-16-07)
- Athletes and Entertainers ("P")
- International Cultural Exchange Visitors ("Q")
- Religious Workers ("R")
- Witnesses and Informants ("S")
- Victims of Trafficking and Violence Protection Act of 2000 (T and U Visas)
- Victims of Human Trafficking ("T")
- Canadian and Mexican Professionals Under NAFTA ("TN")
- Interim U Regulations (September 17, 2007)
- Certain Spouses and Children of Permanent Residents ("V")

If your candidate has a **Green Card**, he/she can go anywhere in the US to work. If your candidate is a **Permanent Resident**, he/she can go anywhere in the US to work. You need to ask the non-US trained candidate his/her visa status at the time they will begin employment. Your candidate may have international training but is a US Citizen. He/she can go anywhere in the US to work.

NUMBERS GAME

Make no mistake about it....recruiting is a Numbers Game. By that I mean that you MUST keep in mind the following to succeed:

Client side: Procuring a client

You will need to make X# (you put in the figure) of phone calls; emails to potential clients to =1 (one) client. i.e., 20 phone calls and/or emails = 1 client who signs the contract.

You have X# of Clients that ='s 1 Good client. A good client is one who is responsive to your calls and emails. A good client contacts your candidate. i.e., 4 clients = 1 good client.

Candidate side: Procuring a candidate

You need to make X# of phone calls or emails to =1 candidate. i.e., 10 phone calls and/or emails =1 candidate who sends you his/her CV.

You need to make X# of phone calls or emails to those candidates to = 1 good candidate who is responsive and placeable. i.e., 5 phone calls and/or emails = 1 good candidate.

Placement side: The actual placement of the candidate with the client.

You need to make X# of phone calls and emails to get 1 candidate for your client. i.e., 20 phone calls and/or emails = 1 good candidate for the client.

You need to have X# of candidates to get 1 phone interview. i.e., 5 candidates = 1 phone interview.

You need to have X# of phone interviews to have 1 Site visit. i.e., 5 phone interviews = 1 site visit.

You need to have X# of Site visits to make 1 placement. i.e., 3 site visits = 1 placement.

If you have a monetary goal for one year, you will know how to work the numbers to achieve that goal. Here is an example.

You want to make $100,000 gross income. Your fees are $20,000 per candidate placed. Breaking that figure down, you need to make 5 full placements (your candidate and your client); ten split placements (you share either candidate or client with a trading partner); or a combination of those. If you have figured that it takes 10 calls to get one candidate; 5 candidates to get one phone interview; 5 phone interviews to get one site visit; 3 site visits to get one placement....then, you know exactly what you need to do to be successful!

You can equate the Numbers Game to building a pyramid. You must, must, must build a strong, wide foundation. We are using example numbers here, so the numbers may vary greatly. But, the end result remains the same. You must have many building blocks or numbers in your base and as you move to the Placement, your numbers become smaller until you have that last number one block which is your Placement!!

GETTING STARTED

Now that you have made the decision to become a **Recruiter,** you need to get started. There are several ways to begin this exciting career:

- Home Office
- Office outside the home
- Join an existing firm
- Become an Internal Recruiter

Home Office

You have decided that you will have your office inside your home. It is important that you have a space that is dedicated to your office. You cannot have the kitchen counter as your office. You are a professional. Your space needs to be professional. Check with your city or town to make sure there are no ordinances prohibiting your office. If you have walk-in traffic (i.e., candidates coming in) you may need to be in the proper zoning. If you have little walk-in traffic, you will probably need to just get a business license.

Select a business name. Your name represents you and your business. Be professional. Although some names might be cute, remember that you are a professional. You may wish to work your name into your business name or you may decide to work your profession into the business name. That is for you to decide. You should probably seek tax advice on whether your name should be Incorporated, LLC, etc. A CPA or tax lawyer can advise you on the best way to proceed.

Register your name with your state of residence. You may need to also apply for a city license.

Office equipment: Desk and chair. Make sure it is something that fits you.

Website: We strongly urge you to either develop a website or have a web designer develop a site for you. Buy a domain name and set up an email account. In today's market, a web presence is very important. Most individuals will never contact you by doing a web search because there are millions of sites out there. But, you can drive individuals to your site by having it listed on any ads you do as well as your business cards, etc.

Computer: You can have a desk top; laptop or both. Get used to being a paperless office. Have things emailed so you can put everything into documents on your computer. You can even have a fax number that comes into your computer. You do not even need a fax machine. (Refer to **Lean Mean Paperless Machine** in this manual)

Fax: In today's market email is taking over faxing. Still, you may want to have a fax number. You can have a fax number on line and never have to install a fax or line inside your office. One service for fax that comes directly into your computer is E-fax which you can find at efax.com.

Phone: Don't use your home line as your business line. You are a professional and you need a separate business line(s). If you have one business line, be sure you have the services of call waiting, forwarding, etc. A cell phone can be used also. You should also invest in a headset or ear bud while you are on the phone. Many times you will be putting notes into your computer while you are talking (i.e., interviewing a client) at the same time, you are putting interview notes into the computer.

Your computer and phone are your business lifelines. As a recruiter you will be on your phone calling clients, candidates, and trading partners constantly. You need to answer your phone in a business manner. Here are two examples:

- **A no-no**: Your business phone rings, you pick it up while you are clanging around in the kitchen and say, "Hello." Tsk, tsk....not professional. Also, do not let your young children answer your business phone. **REMEMBER**...this is your livelihood and it is a business!
- **Correct way**: Your business phone rings and you pick it up. "XYZ Corporation, this is Sam, may I help you?"

Tax issues: Owning your own business also means setting up procedures for filing taxes. Keep all receipts and have a monthly accounting of all of those receipts in your various categories of office equipment, travel, supplies, etc. Remember, you are responsible now for paying your taxes. Be sure to have a system firmly in place. Reconcile your business accounts monthly at the very minimum. Keep accurate records. Also, remember that if you have a home office, you have deductions that apply to that space. Conferring with a good tax lawyer, accountant, or books on the subject will greatly help you.

Office Outside the Home

If you choose to have an office outside the home, you will still need to set it up like your home office. Other considerations for a home office include

Area: Choose an office to fit your needs. If you have candidates or clients coming into your office, you will need an area that is convenient and zoned properly.

Office set-up: If you have that walk-in traffic, you will need to have an office designed to have a waiting area as well as individual office space. If there will be more than one recruiter per office, you will need to allow each recruiter his/her own space with the appropriate equipment as described in the Home Office section.

Break area: You will probably want to have an area that will have some break area amenities such as a coffee pot, small refrigerator, running water, etc. The sky is pretty much the limit in determining your individual office needs.

Join an Existing Firm

If you want to become a recruiter, but are not comfortable with having your own business just yet, you may want to join a larger firm. You find this job in the same manner as locating any other job. Remember, you are a professional and you need to interview as a professional. If you sign a contract or employment agreement, make sure that you read it carefully. You may be signing a non-compete and you need to be aware of this.

Become an Internal Recruiter

This is pretty self explanatory. You apply for; interview for; and get hired by a company or hospital to do their recruiting. You are probably already experienced or you wouldn't have gotten hired to do this job.

GETTING STARTED: WHAT DO I DO NOW?

You have your business and have your office established. Now it is time to get down to the basics. In this manual, you will be taught to be a physician recruiter. Remember, though, the basic elements and principles will apply to many other areas of recruitment.

KNOWLEDGE IS EVERYTHING: In the business of physician recruitment, you can never have too much knowledge. You need to set aside time to familiarize yourself with all terms and aspects of the physician/healthcare field. We have already outlined standard recruitment terms earlier in the manual. Here we will begin to train you as a physician recruiter.

CANDIDATE TERMS

Physician or Doctor: This is a medical professional who has successfully completed his/her healthcare degree. All physicians have already received an undergraduate degree: either a Bachelors in Science or Art. Then, the candidate is accepted into a university or health sciences center to attend 4 more years of medical education. There are two types of physicians MD and DO.

MD: This refers to a Medical Doctor. This candidate has gone to an "allopathic" university and received his/her MD or Medical Degree. Sometimes an International medical graduate will have a degree which is equivalent to an MD, such as an MBBS.

DO: This refers to a Doctor of Osteopathy. This candidate has gone through an "osteopathic" program and received his/her DO degree. The difference between the two involves the educational components. Often a DO will do what is called manipulation. You can get additional information by doing a search engine search on the internet.

Mid-Level Practitioner: This refers to the Physician Assistant, Nurse Practitioner, and CRNA.

Physician Assistant (PA): This is a medical professional who is sometimes referred to as a Mid-Level Practitioner. He/she can take medical histories, examine and diagnose patients, order labs and x-rays, and prescribe treatment. The PA is supervised by a physician.

Nurse Practitioner (NP): This is a medical professional who is sometimes referred to as a Mid-Level Practitioner. He/she is a Registered Nurse who has continued education and has become accredited as a Nurse Practitioner. The NP can generally run a medical office and perform many of the duties of the physician. A licensed physician supervises.

CRNA: This is the Nurse Anesthetist who is also a Mid-Level Practitioner. He/she performs all the duties of an Anesthesiologist from Pre-op to Post Op. (Pre-Op is working with the patient before the patient goes into surgery. Post-Op is working with the patient after surgery). A CRNA may or may not be supervised by an anesthesiologist. This will depend on the location.

USMLE: This examination is required for every physician who wishes to practice in any state or US held territory. This information is extracted from the website: www.usmle.org.
"In the United States and its territories, the individual medical licensing authorities ("state medical boards") of the various jurisdictions grant a license to practice medicine. Each medical licensing authority sets its own rules and regulations and requires passing an examination that demonstrates qualification for licensure. Results of the USMLE are reported to these authorities for use in granting the initial license to practice medicine. The USMLE provides them with a common evaluation system for applicants for initial medical licensure.
The USMLE is sponsored by the Federation of State Medical Boards of the United States, Inc (FSMB), and The National Board of Medical Examiners (NBME). The USMLE assesses a physician's ability to apply knowledge, concepts, and principles, and to demonstrate fundamental patient-centered skills, that are important in health and disease and that constitute the basis of safe and effective patient care. Each of the three Steps of the USMLE complements the others; no Step can stand alone in the assessment of readiness for medical licensure. Because individual medical licensing authorities make decisions regarding use of USMLE results, physicians seeking licensure should contact the jurisdiction where they intend to apply for licensure to obtain complete information. Also, the FSMB can provide general information."

ECFMG: Physicians who attend medical school outside the US or US held territory, are required to take this examination. You can find more information by going to www.ecfmg.org. The following is extracted from that website.
"Medical schools outside the United States and Canada vary in their educational standards and curricula. The purpose of ECFMG Certification is to assess the readiness of graduates of these schools to enter U.S. residency and fellowship programs that are accredited by the Accreditation Council for Graduate Medical Education (ACGME). To be certified by ECFMG, you must pass a series of exams; you must also fulfill ECFMG's medical education credential requirements. These requirements include providing ECFMG with copies of your medical education credentials, which ECFMG will verify directly with your medical school. If you are an international medical graduate and wish to enter an ACGME-accredited residency or fellowship program in the United States, you must be certified by ECFMG before you can enter the program. You must be

certified by ECFMG if you wish to take Step 3 of the three-step United States Medical Licensing Examination (USMLE). ECFMG Certification is also one of the requirements to obtain an unrestricted license to practice medicine in the United States."

Residency: Once a physician completes his/her degree, that physician must go into an approved residency program. The physician decides what specialty he/she wants to practice and applies for residency training. Residency training differs from the prior educational training in two ways: First, the Resident receives a salary which is generally pretty meager. Second, the Resident works in a hospital setting under the tutelage of a skilled physician.

The Resident sees patients and provides all healthcare needs of the patient. The number of years the physician is in residency depends on the specialty. Those years range from 3-5 years. Many times the first year of the doctor's residency is called an Internship. If you hear the word Intern, that refers to the doctor in his/her first year of post graduate training. Most of the time you will hear the term Resident referring to the doctor who is in his/her residency training.

A doctor can be licensed and practice medicine after completing that first year. But, he/she is not eligible for Board Certification.

Sometimes you will see that a doctor is or was a Chief Resident. This is a doctor who has been "elected" or chosen to remain in residency for an extra year. This is an honor and that doctor supervises and trains several residents.

Some international or foreign trained doctors (doctors who have received their MD's from a program outside the US or Puerto Rico) also do an extra year of US training depending on from what country their degree is earned.

Fellowship: After residency is completed some physician/doctors opt to continue training by being accepted into a fellowship. This represents additional training so the doctor can specialize in certain areas. This training is usually an additional one to three years.

Specialty: This refers to the area in which your physician will specialize. The Board of Medical Specialties recognizes the physician specialties listed in the next section. According to the American Board of Medical Specialties (abms.org), these are specialties and subspecialties in which your candidate can practice.

Board Eligible: When a doctor has completed his/her residency and/or fellowship, he/she is "eligible" to take a test which determines if that doctor will qualify to become Board Certified in his/her chosen area of specialty. This test usually is both written and oral. In some cases there is a time limit on how long a physician can be eligible without getting board certified.

Board Certified: A doctor has completed and passed both his written and oral Boards (tests) and is Board Certified in his/her area of specialty. Some specialties receive a Certification. It is important for you to find out if your candidate is Board Eligible (BE) or Board Certified (BC), if your candidate is a practicing physician. If your candidate is a resident, he/she is BE since he/she has not finished training. This can affect a State licensure. Some states require that a physician be Boarded within so many years of training. If not, that physician may be required to take another text (sometimes FLEX). Also, most physicians must be credentialed by a hospital where they will have admitting privileges. Many hospitals require Boards to have been taken within a delegated number of years after training.

Permanent or Locum Tenens: Permanent refers to a full time job for your candidate. Locum Tenens or locums as it is sometimes called refer to the job which is like a substitute. Locums jobs need candidates for fill-in work.

Credentialing/Privileges: Many physicians apply for privileges at one or more hospitals where they will be practicing. The hospital has an individual(s) who does the work necessary to get a doctor Credentialed at that hospital. This is a time consuming process and you as the recruiter are usually not involved in this process. This is a term, though, that you need to know. The physician becomes credentialed at a hospital which gives him/her privileges at that hospital. That means the doctor can see patients in the hospital.

Malpractice: All physicians who practice medicine carry malpractice insurance. Most of the time the practices or hospitals pay this malpractice premium for a designated period of time. You MUST ask your physician candidate if he or she has experienced any malpractice in his/her career. You will need to ask for some details. Remember, you are representing your client and sometimes a physician has too many malpractice issues for you to place that doc. Knowledge is your best bet here. Some specialties require "tail coverage". This coverage is in case the physician has a future lawsuit. Knowing the amount of tail is important when you are moving a physician from one state to another to practice.

Disciplinary Action: This is another critical area for your awareness when interviewing a physician candidate. Always ask a physician candidate about any disciplinary action in which he or she is or was involved. This can include any of the following:

- Licensure restrictions or loss in any state;
- Loss or restricted privileges at any hospital;
- Chemical abuse issues such as alcohol or drug related issues.

Any legal issues that will show up on the National Practitioner Data Bank when becoming credentialed at a hospital is important for you to know. Hospitals access this databank. If a physician has anything that will show up on a data bank inquiry, you must be aware of it. The NPDB is a national databank that provides information to hospitals and clinics about a physician's background. You cannot access this, but you can bet that your client will access it if they want to hire your candidate. So, it is best for you to know everything ahead of time. Clients can overlook some issues, but they need to be aware of them.

National Practitioner Data Bank: Any action against a physician is recorded on this data bank. Your client will access this if your candidate is considered for hire. Always ask your candidate if there is anything that will appear on this data bank. If so, have your candidate describe the action.

State Licensure: A doctor or Mid-Level Practitioner must apply for and receive a license from each State in which he/she practices. Each State has a licensure board usually called The Board of Healing Arts or such. You need to check your candidate's license to be sure it is current and has no restrictions. An easy way to do this is to go to the website http://www.fsmb.org/directory_smb.html and click on the State in which you wish to check licensure. You also need to be aware that it can take 3-8 months for a physician to become licensed. It simply depends on each State.

Family Needs: Remember that it is not illegal to ask a candidate about family issues and needs. This is an important area, but if a candidate does not wish to answer anything related to this area, that is his or her prerogative. But, for our purposes, we will assume the candidate will answer questions here. You can explain to a candidate that knowing family needs helps you to make the right match. Some of the following are helpful areas:

- Hobbies and Interests: This can be things like sailing, opera, golfing, etc.

- Wife, husband, or Significant Other Occupation: It may be important to know that the spouse is, for example, a chemical engineer in the oil industry. You know that your spot in non oil region is not appropriate.
- Children Needs: This can be important if the family has a specific education need for their child. Maybe one of the children has an outside activity that you need to address.
- Other Family Needs: Maybe another relative lives with them and has a special need that you can address. The family may also have religious or cultural needs that will need to be accommodated.

Remember, you want a good match of candidate, job, and community. Family needs are very important.

Geographics: This is a very important interviewing area. You will ask your candidate where he or she wants to relocate. If the candidate tells you that he/she is OPEN, don't accept it right away. Continue to narrow his/her geographic scope down. You can do this by asking if he/she will go to all states. If the answer is yes, ask if he/she will go to western Kansas; northern North Dakota; rural Mississippi; Alaskan Yukon...you get the idea. Unless a candidate is on a J-1 visa, that candidate is not necessarily OPEN. If the candidate is of a specialty that requires a large medical center, then you will know that metro areas will probably be the only options. You need to find out what State(s) the candidate will consider. You need to find out what population size the candidate will consider.

Sometimes you need to be a bit of an investigator. Certain things will give you some geographic ideas:

- Hobbies: i.e. sailing (candidate will need to be close to sailing water)
- Where did candidate and family grow up? Wife is from Indianapolis; candidate is from Indianapolis; went to Medical School in Indiana. Hmmmmm....
- What attracts candidate to states of choice?

These elements will be discussed several times in this manual. After the Specialty Definitions, we will discuss Contracts, Job Orders and Candidate Profiles. These items are your mainstay. They are what make you a successful recruiter.

SPECIALTY DEFINITIONS

Listed are the specialty names and common abbreviations. *B* means the physician can be Board Certified in this and *C* means the physician can have a special Certificate in this.

Allergy & Immunology (AI) B: Diagnoses and treats allergic conditions relating to the skin, respiratory tract and sinuses.

Anesthesiology (AN) B: Administers anesthesia and monitors patients under anesthesia during surgery and other medical procedures. Areas of subspecialty under Anesthesiology include Critical Care Medicine (CC) C; Pain Medicine C; Hospice and Palliative Care C.

Colon and Rectal Surgery (CRS) B: Specializes in colon and rectal diseases.

Dermatology (D) B: Specializes in the management of diseases related to the skin, nails, and hair. Subspecialties of Dermatology can include Dermatopathology C: Studies tissue and Pediatric Dermatology C**:** Works with children under the age of 16.

Emergency Medicine (EM) B: Diagnoses and treats conditions needing immediate attention, including illness, trauma, and industrial, sports, and occupational accidents. Subspecialties under Emergency Medicine include Hospice and Palliative Care C; Medical Toxicology C; Pediatric Emergency Medicine C; Sports Medicine C; and Underseas and Hyperbaric Medicine C.

Family Practice (FP) B: A family practice physician treats patients of all ages for a variety of illnesses and helps to maintain general healthcare. Subspecialties under Family Practice can include Adolescent Medicine C**:** post pediatric and pre-adult; Geriatric Medicine C: Senior medicine; Hospice and Palliative Care C; Obstetrics C: Child delivery and women's health issues; Sleep Medicine C; and Sports Medicine C.

Internal Medicine (IM) B: An internist diagnoses and treats general medical disorders of adults such as diabetes, high blood pressure, heart disease, emphysema, and cancer. A subspecialty of Internal Medicine is Adolescent Medicine C**.**

Cardiovascular Disease (Card) C: Invasive, non-invasive, interventional Cardiology: diagnoses and treats diseases of the heart and blood vessels.

Cardiac Electrophysiology (EP) C: Cardiology specializing in Electrophysiology

Critical Care Medicine (CC) (Hospitalists are this many times) **C:** This physician generally follows the patient in the critical care unit.

Endocrinology, Diabetes, and Metabolism (ENDO) C: Treats disorders of the endocrine system, including the thyroid and adrenal glands, which help control the body's metabolic activity. Conditions include diabetes, nutritional and metabolic disorders, and bone disorders such as osteoporosis.

Gastroenterology (GI) C: A gastroenterologist specializes in the diagnosis, treatment of diseases of the stomach, intestines, and related areas such as esophagus, intestines, liver, gallbladder, and pancreas.

Geriatric Medicine (G) C: Older adult medicine.

Hemotology (Hem) C: Blood related diagnosis and treatment.

Hospice & Palliative Medicine (HPM) C: Pain treatment and end of life treatment.

Infectious Disease (ID) C: Diagnosis, cause, and treatment of contagious disease.

Interventional Cardiology (CDINT) C: Uses catheters and other devices to restore blood flow to the heart without the need for major surgery.

Medical Oncology (ONC) C: Diagnosis and treatment of Cancer.

Nephrology (NEP) C: Diagnosing and treating problems with kidneys, high blood pressure, fluid retention and electrolyte imbalance.

Pulmonolgy Disease (PUD) C: Diagnoses and treats disorders of the lungs and chest cavity, such as asthma, bronchitis, emphysema, pneumonia. Many times the PUD is also a Critical Care physician.

Rheumatology (RHU) C: Diagnoses and treats arthritis, bone disorders, and connective tissue disease.

Medical Genetics (MG) (Seldom will you ever need this) **B:** Study of genetics.

Neurological Surgery (NS) B: Neurosurgeon provides neurological services including surgical treatment of cervical and lumbar spine problems, brain tumors, neurovascular problems, and peripheral nerve problems.

Nuclear Medicine (NM) C: Uses radioactive substances, called radionuclides or tracers, to create images of the body and its organs.

Obstetrics and Gynecology (OBG) B: Provides care during pregnancy, labor, and childbirth, and also diagnosis and treats the female reproductive system.

Gynecology Oncology (GYN-ONC) C: Treats cancer of the female reproductive system.

Ophthalmology (OPH) B: Treats eye disorders, including injuries, infections, tumors, and cataracts.

Orthopaedic Surgery (ORS) B: (also spelled orthopedic): Treats skeletal abnormalities including injuries or diseases of the bones, joints, spine, and muscles. Subspecialties include Hand Surgery C; Spine Surgery; Total Joints; Sports Medicine C.

Otolaryngology (OTO) B: (also called **ENT** or Ear, Nose, and Throat) Specializes in the treatment of disease and injuries affecting the ear, nose, and throat. Subspecialties include Pediatric Otolaryngology C and Maxial Facial Plastic Surgery.

Pathology (PTH) B: Studies tissue, organs, and bodily fluids under a microscope to diagnose diseases. Subspecialties include Anatomical Pathology B; Clinical Pathology B; Forensic Pathology C; Dermatopathology C; Pediatric Pathology C.

Pediatrics (PED) B: Treats diseases and helps maintain the general health of children from birth through the teenage years. Just about every adult and adolescent specialty will have a Pediatric specialty so we won't list them again here. (Check Specialty Board Listings)

Physical Medicine and Rehabilitation (Physiatrist) (PM&R) B: Diagnosis, treatment, and care of physical disabilities resulting from a variety of medical conditions. These can include musculoskeletal disorders, neurological disease, cardiac-respiratory problems, amputations, and chronic pain. A subspecialty is Pain Medicine.

Plastic Surgery (PS) B: Deals with the repair, reconstruction, or replacement of physical defects of form or function involving the skin, musculoskeletal system, craniomaxillofacial structures, hand, extremities, breast and trunk, external genitalia, or cosmetic enhancement of these areas of the body. Subspecialties include Hand Plastics; Face and Neck; Cosmetic.

Preventive Medicine (PRVM) B: Studies disease and injury prevention.

Occupational Medicine (OM) B: Treats job related accidents. Subspecialties include Medical Toxicology C; Aerospace B; Underseas C; Public Health B.

Psychiatry (PSY) and Neurology (N) B: Two separate physicians: The *Psychiatrist* diagnoses and treats emotional illnesses as well as physical ailments with significant emotional aspects. *Neurology:* Specializes in the diagnosis and treatment of the nervous system, including the brain, spinal cord and nerves, while a physician specializing in sleep medicine focuses on sleep and sleep disorders. Subspecialties include Pediatric Neurology B; Pain Medicine C; Sleep Medicine C; Adult Psychiatry B; Child and Adolescent Psychiatry C; Geriatric Psychiatry C; Forensic Psychiatry C. (Check Specialty Boards for less used areas.)

Radiology (R) B: Uses x-rays, radiant dyes, nuclear medicine, ultrasound, and magnetic resonance imaging to "photograph" the skeletal, arterial and soft tissue areas of the body to diagnose and treat disease or injury. A subspecialty includes Diagnostic Radiology B.

Radiation Oncology (RO) B: Uses Radiation to treat cancer. Subspecialties include Nuclear Radiology C; Pediatric Radiology C; Vascular and Interventional Radiology C. Surgery B: Specializes in the diagnosis and treatment of diseases through surgical treatment.

General Surgery (GS) C: Diagnoses and treats all ages through surgery.

Vascular Surgery (VS) B: Specializes in the diagnosis and treatment of diseases of the arterial, venous, and lymphatic systems, exclusive of those components intrinsic to the heart and intracranial vessels. (Check Specialty Boards for less used areas)

Thoracic Surgery (CTS) B: (referred to as Cardiothoracic); Specializes in diagnosis and treatment of diseases of the lungs.

Urology (U) B: Diagnoses and treats diseases of the urinary tract.

For more information on Specialties and Subspecialties go to www.abms.org. We also have detailed explanations of the specialties in the Medical Specialties section.

CONTINGENCY VS RETAINED CONTRACTS

There are two types of Permanent contracts that recruiters use: Contingency and Retained. If you provide Locums physicians, you will also need a Locums contract.

Contingency Contract

This is a contract that you send to your client. In this contract you state that a fee is owed contingent upon placing a candidate with the client. You will outline your fee; what you will do for that fee; what the client is responsible for doing; and what you guarantee. You should have a standard contingency for your firm. Some clients have their own contingency and insist that you sign theirs. That is not at all unusual. You will need to read it carefully and agree to their terms. A standard fee payment schedule in most contingency agreements is half of your fee is due within ten days of the candidate signing the Client contract. The other half is due when the Candidate begins practice. It is up to you to outline your term. Both you and your Client sign this contract.

Retained Contract

This is a contract that you send to your client. In this contract you state a fee that retains your services. This fee is paid either upfront or monthly depending on how you arrange the contract. The client expects you to provide the service that you state you will provide. For that, you client provides you with either start-up money or money that means you will provide the physician candidate. In addition to the retainer, the client usually pays a placement fee when the physician signs the contract and commences practicing for your client.

Two sample contingency contracts follow. A retained contract is similar to the following contracts. It, though, includes the monthly retainer and that amount varies according to the client.

Contracts are varied and can be streamlined to fit your purpose. The important elements of a contract state what you are contracted to provide; what is your fee is for this service; how this fee is to be paid; what your guarantee is for this service; what your client is expected to provide; what state jurisdiction will be in case of lawsuit; etc. You want to make sure you are covered in any conceivable scenario.

Example Contract #1

CONTINGENCY AGREEMENT

Date: January 1, 2000

It is agreed that XYZ Hospital hereinafter referred to as CLIENT, located in Louisiana, contracts with ABC and Associates, located in Missouri, hereinafter referred to as COMPANY, to conduct a search for placement of qualified candidates in the specialty of physician.

1. **Term of the Agreement**: This agreement becomes effective upon written acceptance by both parties and shall remain in force for the term of one year, although either party has the right to terminate this agreement for any reason prior to the expiration of such term with ten days written notice. However, unless either party notifies the other in writing of its intention not to continue the agreement at least ten days before the expiration of this term, the agreement shall be automatically renewed and extended for an additional period of one year. Further renewals pursuant to this procedure will occur at the expirations of any extension period.

2. **Responsibilities of Parties**: COMPANY will extend its best effort to identify and recruit qualified candidates who meet the criteria specified by CLIENT. CLIENT agrees to respond to COMPANY in a timely manner concerning all business related to this agreement. CLIENT shall keep COMPANY informed, in a timely manner, of all developments affecting this agreement including all discussions with candidates. CLIENT agrees to pay all candidate interview expenses.

3. **Placement Fee**: CLIENT agrees to pay COMPANY a placement fee of $22,000 per candidate referred by COMPANY and said candidate has not previously been in personal contact with CLIENT for a period of six months from the date of Company's referral and candidate referred by COMPANY is hired or retained in any capacity within two years of the date of referral whether as employee, consultant or independent contractor by CLIENT or any of its affiliates or in the event CLIENT refers the candidate to another employer who hires or retains the candidate. Fees will be billed when an offer is made and accepted, with payment terms as follows: one-half of the fee will be payable within fourteen business days of the candidate's contractual signing date, with the balance being payable within fourteen business days of the candidate's start date.

4. **Replacement Guarantee**: Should the candidate referred by COMPANY leave CLIENT within ninety days of candidate's start date, COMPANY will replace said candidate for the same position with an equally qualified replacement accepted by CLIENT. This replacement guarantee shall only be valid if:

- COMPANY is notified in writing of said separation within five working days; and
- The fee is paid in full within fourteen days of candidate's start date.

5. Company has 180 days to replace candidate. If Company provides qualified candidates and Client does not hire candidate, replacement guarantee is null after 180 days.

In accordance with federal and state equal opportunity laws, COMPANY will refer all qualified candidates without regard to race, color, national origin, sex, age, physical handicap or medical condition.

Any disputes between COMPANY and CLIENT will be governed by the laws of the state of Missouri.

Should it become necessary for COMPANY to employ a collection agency or attorney to collect the principal, interest and all other lawful charges, the cost and expenses of collection, including but not limited to reasonable attorney's fees and court costs, shall be paid by CLIENT.

Acceptance of any of Company's referred candidates for interviews shall indicate full agreement with the above terms.

______________________	______________________
Company	Client
______________________	______________________
Signature	Signature
______________________	______________________
Name Printed and Date	Name Printed and Date

Example Contract #2

REFERRAL AGREEMENT

This Agreement is entered into by and between (name of hospital or clinic recruiting) (hereinafter referred to as "Client") and ABC Corp (hereinafter referred to as ABC).

WHEREAS, Client is looking for a physician and/or mid-level provider to fill a position in the clients service area (examples: but not limited to, join a medical practice in the area/start a medical practice/be an employee/join the clients medical staff or join other medical providers in the area); and

WHEREAS, ABC is in the business, among other things, of finding and placing providers when employment opportunities occur; and

WHEREAS, Client desires to employ ABC on a contingent referral fee basis to find and place a provider in the above-referenced facility and/or community area;

Now, therefore, the parties agree as follows:

1. Client agrees to use ABC as its agent under the terms of this agreement for finding and placing a medical provider, and ABC agrees to conduct its best efforts to find and place a medical provider for the client.

2. In the event that a provider is accepted by Client for the above positions and said provider was referred to Client and/or became aware of the opening through the efforts of ABC, then Client agrees to pay ABC a referral fee of:

PROVIDER FEE SCHEDULE

GENERALPRACTICE	$20,000
PSYCHIATRY	$22,000
FAMILY PRAC no OB	$22,000
NEUROLOGY	$22,000
FAMILY PRAC W/OB	$22,000
ENT-OPHTHALMOLOGY	$22,000
GENERAL INT MED	$22,000
ORTHOPEDICS	$22,000
PEDIATRICS	$22,000
NEURORADIOLOGY	$22,000

RADIOLOGY	$22,000
SURG & RAD ONCOLOGY	$22,000
EMERGENCY DEPT	$22,000
ICU/ TRAMATOLOGY	$22,000
GEN/VAS/TH SURG	$22,000
OB/GYN	$22,000
INT MED, FELLOW	$22,000
NEUROSURGERY	$22,000
CARDIAC SURGERY	$22,000
DEPT CHIEF/DIRECTOR	$24,000
ANESTHESIOLOGY	$22,000
PHYSICIAN ASST/CRNA	$15,000
NEPHROLOGY/UROLOGY	$22,000
CERT NURSE PRAC.	$15,000

LOCUM TENENS COVERAGE: $75 PER DAY AND YOU ARRANGE PROVIDERS SALARY

3. The phrase "through the efforts" shall include but is not limited to:
a. The provider was identified to the Client by ABC; or
b. The provider acknowledges that he/she first became aware of the opening with the Client, through the efforts of ABC; or
c. ABC arranged the first contact, or interview, or meeting between Client and the provider.

4. We will replace any person hired through us who terminates or is terminated from his or her position of employment within sixty (60) days from the date the candidate commences said employment, provided the client notifies us, in writing, of all the facts relating to the termination of said employment within five (5) business days after said termination, unless this person is terminated because the client has insufficient work for the candidate. This guarantee is provided to allow you to satisfy yourself that the candidate has the requisite experience and qualifications, and that information provided by the candidate and other sources, directly or through us is accurate. This guarantee shall be your sole remedy.

5. Candidates are referred to you in confidence, for use in your immediate service area, and are not to be entered into a corporate data base. Should you refer, or otherwise identify, such a candidate to another company which hires the candidate, you and the hiring company shall be responsible for payment of our fee.

6. Client is obligated to pay the contingent referral fee to ABC whether or not the employment of the candidate occurs before or after the exclusive term of the Agreement.

7. We will invoice you for our services when the candidate accepts employment. Our terms are "FIFTY PERCENT (50%) of NET-DUE ON THE DATE THE CANDIDATE SIGNS A CONTRACT AND FIFTY PERCENT (50%) OF NET-DUE ON THE DATE THE CANDIDATE COMMENCES EMPLOYMENT." The guarantee referred to in item number four (4) is valid only if we receive payment of 50% of our service fee, in full, within thirty (30) days from the date the candidate signs a contract and 50% of our service fee, in full, within thirty (30) days from the date candidate commences employment. THE TERMS OF THIS CONTRACT WILL BE ENFORCED. In the event of failure of client to pay this contingent referral fee, or any portion thereof, to ABC, such delinquent amount shall accrue interest at the rate of 12% per annum from the start date of employment of the physician. Should it become necessary for ABC to employ a collection agency or attorney to collect the principal, interest and all other lawful charges, the cost and expenses of collection, including but not limited to reasonable attorney's fees and court costs, shall be paid by client. In the event of legal action to enforce or interpret the terms of this Agreement, venue and jurisdiction of such legal action shall be in (Your area of residence).

______________________	______________________
Company	Client
______________________	______________________
Signature	Signature
______________________	______________________
Name Printed and Date	Name Printed and Date

GETTING THE CANDIDATE

To fill your job order you will need a candidate. There are numerous ways to acquire your candidate to fill you need. I will list a few here.

1. Apply to and belong to a network of recruiters to get shared candidates. Go to www.allianceofmedicalrecruiters.com and click Join AMR. This is one network, but you can probably search the web for others.
2. Talk to your local doctor and simply find out if he/she knows anyone look for a job. Referrals can be a great source.
3. Advertise on a job board on the web. There are many sites for jobs but you should look for healthcare or medical boards rather than those that are all inclusive. You should price the boards in order to advertise according to your budget.
4. Advertise in medical journals such as JAMA; New England Journal of Medicine, Unique Opportunities, and other specialty journals. These ads can be productive, but you need to check costs here as well.
5. Attend medical conventions healthcare job fairs, and other healthcare related meetings.
6. Buy lists of potential candidates. A web search will provide lots of sources.
7. Subscribe to services like DOC Project through The Alliance of Medical Recruiters. This service sends candidates directly to you email.
8. Visit residency programs and speak with residency directors. You may be able to post your jobs as well as talk to residents.
9. Cold calls. Find candidates through these various sources and just pick up the phone and call! You never know when you'll find a candidate who is looking to make a career change.

These are just a few ways to get a candidate and you will probably think of many other ways to access a good candidate. After you get the candidate, you must do a thorough interview of that candidate. Following will be critical information for you as you interview your candidates.

CANDIDATE PROFILE

A candidate profile is a form you use when you interview a candidate. Obviously, the important components will include:

- Name and title (MD or DO)
- Specialty and subspecialty if it applies
- Address
- Phone numbers: Home, Office (if they can be contacted at the office), pager, cell
- Email address
- Current licenses and certifications held
- Inactive licenses
- Geographic areas of interest
- Population sizes
- Practice needs
- Community needs
- Any malpractice, licensure and privilege problems or restrictions; chemical dependence issues
- Copy of current CV
- Visa issues
- Availability
- Call the state(s) where the physician is licensed and verify that license. (make notes in your candidate's file)
- Ask if the candidate has references ready for you when they are needed.

Below is a detailed candidate profile. You use this to get to know your candidate so you can make the best match with a client or trading partner. Some candidates do not have the time for you to ask everything. So, make sure you get the basics and any more that time will allow. Make sure you review the form before you contact the candidate. Some questions may only apply to residents and some may only apply to practicing candidates. When possible, get the CV before you do conduct the candidate interview. You may need to ask questions based on the information on their CV. Remember, you need a good candidate profile to make a good match.

ALWAYS GET THE CV!

Example Interview Form

COMPREHENSIVE SCREEN FORM

Name: ____

MD or DO?: __________

Address: ____

____

Home Phone: ______________________________

Cell Phone: ______________________________

Office Phone: ______________________________

Pager: ______________________________

Email Address: ______________________________

Current Practice setting: Resident? ________ Fellow? _________

If Practicing are you Solo?_________Group?________Partner?______

Other? ______________________

Are you a US Citizen? ___________

If not, are you on a visa? (Be specific) ______________________________________

____

____

Estimated date you are you available to begin a new practice? __________________

What special procedures do you perform/Niches? _____________________________

____

____

____

How many patients do you see each day? ______________________________

What are your salary expectations? ______________________________

What are you currently making in salary? ____________________

How long have you been at this practice? ____________________

Why do you wish to leave? ____________________

____

____

Where and when did you practice prior to this? ____________________

____

Why did you leave that practice? ____________________

____

Educational and training information is usually covered in the CV so you don't need to expound on it here.

Any abnormalities with training or education (i.e. gaps in time, changes in residency?)

____

Any gaps of time between jobs? If yes, why? Be specific: ____________________

____

____

In what states do you have current or lapsed licenses? ____________________

____

Are you Board Certified? __________ Year __________

Are you Board Eligible? __________ If NO, do you plan on Certification?______

Have you experienced any malpractice? Get details.____________________

____

____

Have you had any license or hospital privilege denied, revoked or suspended? Get details. ____________________

____

Have you now or in the past had any alcohol or drug related problems? Get details.

____

____

Do you have anything that will show up on a Data Bank Inquiry? Get details.

____

____

Relocation Preferences

What states are of interest to you and your family? ______________________

____

What states would you not consider? _______________________________

____

Why are these states of interest? ____________________________________

____

What population sizes are of interest to you? ___________________________

____

What activities do you and your family or significant other enjoy that will help me screen opportunities? ____

____

Do you have a spouse or significant other who will need an occupation? __________

____

Do you have children and if so, what type of school and activity do we need to consider? ____

____

Practice Preference

What motivates you professionally as you seek an opportunity? ________________

____

What type of practice do you seek? (i.e.: employed, hospitalist, solo, group, partnership, academic) ________________________________

____

What work schedule and call coverage interests you? ________________

____

From a financial standpoint, what do you need to make an opportunity work for you?

(Yearly income; Production; partnership, etc) ________________

____

____

Do you have your CV in with any other hospital, practice, or recruiters so that I will not duplicate your efforts? (Try to get names and details.) ________________

____

____

Do you have any colleagues who are also looking for opportunities? Could you give me the name and contact information? ________________

____

____

Finish your Interview:

- Please email or fax your CV to me. When can I expect to receive it?
- I will email you immediately so that you will have my email address.
- Thank you and I look forward to working with you.

JOB ORDERS

There are two important elements in recruiting: Job Orders and Candidate Profiles. We have discussed the Candidate Profile. In this section we will discuss the job order.

In order to have a Job Order, you must have a Client. Getting a client is a basic recruiting measure. In healthcare recruiting, having a hospital database is essential. You can buy a Hospital Phone Book which is available through Douglas Publications or you can do what many recruiters do and that is a little "leg work" on the Internet. Perform an Internet search for hospital listings and you can access hospitals in any state. Call your local hospitals and clinics. If you use the Internet search, be sure to keep a good record of who is contacted and what is the result. An example is below:

XYZ Hospital, Wichita, Kansas.
Phone 555 555-5555:
Physician recruiter is Roy Jones.
5-22-08: Left Message

ABC Hospital, Pittsburg, Kansas.
Phone 555 444-4444.
Physician Recruiter is Tom Johnson.
5-22-08: He asked for a copy of contingency agreement. Emailed it same day.

Accurate records are important so you can go back and retry someone, or follow up. We suggest that you set up a file or notepad on your computer in which to keep and access these notes.

PHONE CALL PROTOCOL

The following is an example strategy when contacting potential clients.

1. Dial the hospital number and ask for the Physician Recruiter. If there is no such office, ask for Administration and then ask for the individual who does the physician recruiting.

   "Yes, may I speak with the individual in charge of physician recruiting? Could you tell me the name of that person, please?" Be sure to record the name.

2. Introduce yourself.

   "Hello, my name is Sally Smith with The Smith Group. I am a physician recruiter and am working with a physician who is looking to relocate to your area. Do you work with outside recruiters?"

   Answer: "Yes, I do. Could you tell me your fee?"

   "Absolutely. We are a contingency firm and our standard fee is $22,000 with half upon signing and half upon start date. May I send you our contingency contract for your review?" Be sure to get the recruiter's email address and their direct line.

3. Attach your contract agreement to an email and send it out as soon after speaking with the recruiter as possible. Once that contract is accepted and signed, then it is time to get a job order.

4. Follow-up with that internal recruiter the next day if you have not received the signed contract and ask if there are any questions you can answer. Continue follow-up until you have the signed contract.

5. If you have made the decision to become a "retained firm," you will still need to follow the same steps.

Alternate scenario:

Potential client says: "We have our own contingency."

You: "Could you please forward that to me by email and I will get it back to you quickly."

Once you've received this facility contingency, review it carefully to make sure you are willing to abide by it. If so, electronically sign it and send it back (electronic signatures are discussed in the paperless section at the end of the manual). Contract is signed and now it is time for you to get a good and complete Job Order.

GETTING THE JOB ORDER

1. Go to your client's website if they have one and get preliminary information that is on that site. It is also important to do preliminary research on the location. This impresses the client and makes the job order easier for you.

2. Call your Internal Recruiter and get the job details. An example follows:

   ABC Hospital, Pittsburg KS. Internal Recruiter if Tom Johnson.

   "Hi, Tom, this is Sally Smith. I am so excited that we have the executed contract and I can get to work for you. Do you have a few minutes so I can get a complete job order?

3. Once the client has time to give a job order, do your best to answer the following questions. The client may not have all the answers at that time. For these questions, we'll use a Family Practice (FP) position as an example:

   - What kind of job situation is this (i.e., employee, solo, partnership, etc)?
   - What is your salary range for this doc?
   - Will you pay benefits and what are those benefits?
   - Will you pay moving expenses and is there a set amount?
   - Do you have loan forgiveness?
   - Will you accept both MD and DO candidates?
   - Will you look at a resident?
   - Will you accept an IMG? If so, can you sponsor any visas?
   - Are there any community dynamics that will help me screen candidates?
   - How many other FP's are in the community?
   - Do they all have privileges at your hospital?
   - Do your FP's do OB?
   - What is the call coverage for this FP?
   - Is there a good referral base of specialists for this FP?
   - What is the service area of the hospital? (This figure will be different than the town population)
   - Are there any politics about which I need to be aware?
   - What are the selling points of your community and hospital?

These are just a few of the questions you can ask to get a good job order. Below is the basic information you will need for a job order. An example job order form follows. You can adjust this to fit your needs. Thorough, complete job and community profiles will help you make a good candidate match.

BASIC JOB ORDER INFORMATION

Client Name: Get the exact legal name of the client. You will need this for your contract also.

Client Address including zip: You may need to get both physical address and mailing address if they are different.

Client Representative and Title: This is the person with whom you will be working. It is sometimes helpful to get the name of that person's administrative assistant.

Client Phone Number: Get your contact's direct line.

Client Cell Number: Get this if client will give it to you.

Client Email Address: Ask the client if he/she likes communicating through email.

Client website address: Ask client if he/she posts jobs or related marketing information on their business website.

Type of client: Is this a hospital or a private practice

If Hospital: Number of beds
Number of physicians on staff
Level Trauma
Any other pertinent hospital information

If Private Practice: Number of physicians on staff
Number of mid-levels on staff
Breakdown of specialties
Hospital(s) where patients are seen

Specialty Needed: Ask if there is any subspecialty training needed. Also, see if the subspecialty needs to do any extra duties such as Emergency Medicine call.

Type of Practice: There are several types of practices in which a physician can be placed. Sometimes these overlap. You need to find out what this job entails.

- Employed: Will the hospital or practice employ the physician and what environment will the physician be placed.
- MSG: Multi-specialty group which is a group of physicians of varied practices. You may need to find out what specialties are in this MSG.
- SSG: Single specialty group which is a group of like physicians (i.e. FPs). You will want to ask if the physicians have a good referral base.

- Academic: Are there teaching opportunities with this practice?
- Solo: Is the physician going to be on his/her own? What will the hospital do to provide assistance to get the practice successful?
- Partnership: How many years to partnership?
- Hospitalist: This individual admits and follows patients in the hospital.

Call coverage: Find out how call coverage is shared. If your client says 1 in 4, that means that your candidate will be on call every 4th day and typically every 4th weekend. Is the call only from home or does the doctor go to the hospital? If the hospital has a Hospitalist program, the call may much lighter so ask if there is a Hospitalist program.

City Population: City population is important, but proximity to larger metro areas and its amenities (i.e. airport, shopping, and entertainment) might be just as important.

Service area population: Service area will be larger than the city population and represent potential patient draw area.

Salary or Net Income Guarantee: There is usually a range here. The difference between a salary and NIG, or Net Income Guarantee, is that the NIG after the 1st or 2nd year is dependent upon collections. Your client can explain this to you.

Benefits Package: The client can explain the benefits which usually include but are not limited to Insurance, retirement, CME (Continued Medical Education), vacation, etc.

Loan Repayment: Have the client explain what this entails if they offer this. Many doctors want an area that helps them pay their educational loans which are usually quite significant. Sometimes this feature will make or break a placement.

Depending on the specialty, you may need to ask different questions. Below is a detailed order form. You can amend this to meet your need. Remember, complete as much of this form as you can ahead of time through your own research before talking to the client.

Example Job Order Form

Job Order

Client Name: ____

Address: ____

Contact Name: ____

Office Phone: ____________________ Cell phone:____________________

Email address: ____

Specialty Needed: ____

Any special procedures required?: ______________________________

Accept MD?_______DO?_______ IMG?_______ Residents?________ Visas?_______

Any special requirements or wants with this job?______________________

____

____

Community

Town population: __________________ Service area: ______________________

Closest metro area? ______________________________________

Community amenities? _____________________________________

____

Economy?____

Primary industries?____

Website for community?____________________________________

Practice Information

Type of practice? ____

How many docs are in the practice? ___________________________________

How many of this specialty are in the area? ______________________________

Call coverage? ____
(If the specialty is Hospitalist, Emergency Medicine, or Urgent Care, you will need to get specific about the hours and schedule.)

Who is the primary doctor or administrator who will be working with the candidate?
____

How long has this need existed? ____________________________________

Is this to replace a doctor? ____

Why did the doctor leave? ____

What is the payor mix? Medicare?________ Medicaid?_______ HMO?_______

Self Pay?________ Insurance?_________

Financial Information

What is the salary or net income guarantee range?_________________________

Productivity? ____

Signing Bonus? ____

Benefits? (Get details)____

____

Loan Repayment? ____

Vacation? ____

CME (Continuing Medical Education) allowance? ___________________________

Hospital Information

Name of hospital(s) (may differ from client name):

____

Hospital website?______________________________

Number of beds?__________ For Profit?_______ Non Profit?__________

Recent renovations? ____________________________

ICU/CCU number of beds?____________________________

Psychiatric number of beds?__________________________

Trauma level?________________________________

Number of Operating Room suites?______________________

Specialty amenities in OR (i.e. Da Vinci Robot)? __________________

____

Level of Nursery?______________________________

Any procedures not done?___________________________

If so, where do they go?___________________________

(Depending on the specialty, you will ask about the number of procedures monthly for that specialty.)

Are there any other selling points you can tell me? __________________

____

____

____

____

PUTTING IT ALL TOGETHER

You now have the basics for being a successful recruiter.

- ✓ You know the healthcare lingo!
- ✓ You have Contracts
- ✓ With contracts, you have Clients
- ✓ You have Job orders to fill
- ✓ You have candidates

Now it is time to put these all together and make the placement!

SCREEN AND SUBMIT

You will now screen your candidates and/or trading partner candidates to see if they will match your job. Let's say you have John Doe who fits the Family Practice job you have for XYZ Hospital. Before you send Dr. Doe, you must do the following:

*Call Dr. Doe to make sure he is interested in your job. Give him the details and get his permission to submit his CV to your client. Email him the details and a reminder that you spoke and you are sending his CV to your client.

*Call or email your client and clear the name. Once your client requests the CV, immediately send the CV as an email attachment and get a return receipt. Make notes in your file.

*Wait 24 hours and call your client to make sure they are interested in your candidate. Find out when the client intends to call your candidate.

*Call and/or email your candidate and give him/her the update.

If you got your candidate from a trading partner, keep the partner apprised of all activity.

TELEPHONE AND SITE INTERVIEWS

You may be part of this process. Follow-up begins to be crucial here. Find out when your client speaks with your doctor. Follow-up with both the Client and the Candidate to find out how they felt the telephone interview went. Get three potential visit dates from your Candidate.

Assist your Client with the Site Visit date. Usually your client will set this up and send the itinerary to your Candidate.

After the Site Visit, immediately assess the interest level from both your Client and your Candidate. Now, begins the crucial part of the entire process.

CLOSE THE DEAL

Your candidate has interviewed with your client. Now, you hit it hard.

- Call the candidate and assess his/her interest. Find out any information that the candidate needs.
- Call the client and assess the interest. Give the client feedback you got from the candidate.
- Urge the client to send the candidate a contract for review.
- Urge the candidate to review the contract quickly.
- You will be on the phone with both the candidate and client to facilitate the contract.
- GET THE CONTRACT SIGNED BY YOUR CANDIDATE.
- GET THE CONTRACT SIGNED BY YOUR CLIENT.
- Bill the client.
- After the candidate starts work, bill the client for the second half.

It is good to maintain follow-up with both the candidate and the client during the guarantee period. Don't bug them, but you want to make sure the deal stays solid.

SUMMARY

This timeline depicts what you should expect in a typical placement scenario. Sometimes you will have a candidate for whom you are trying to find a job, and sometimes you will have a client who is asking you to find candidates. Either way, you will see this same basic progression.

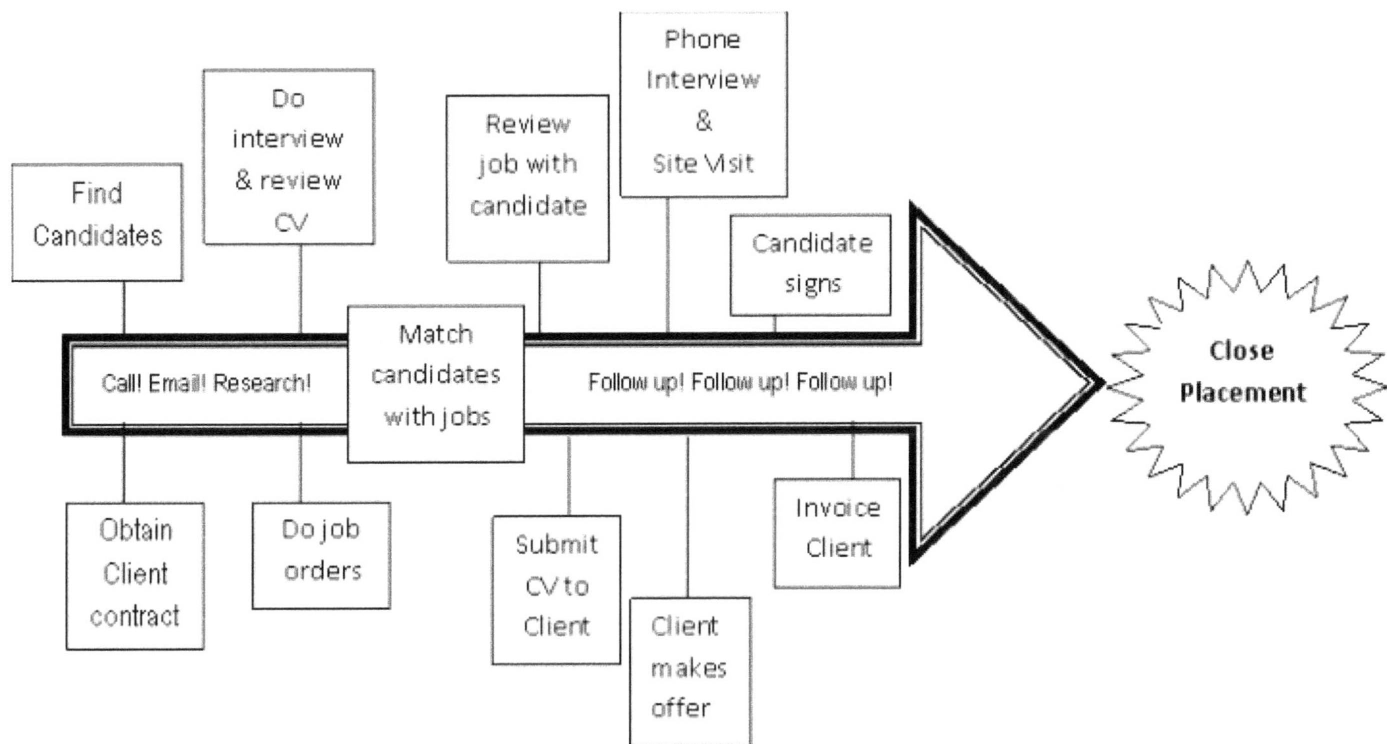

You are on your way to being a successful physician recruiter. It takes persistence and follow-through!

SPLIT BUSINESS: ETHICS AND ETIQUETTE

Split business is when you, the recruiter accepts a candidate or supplies a candidate to another recruiter in another recruitment firm. We have touched on this but need to elaborate since split business is an important element in our industry.

Ethics by definition is a set of principles of correct conduct. The rules of conduct are recognized in respect to a particular class of human actions or a particular group such as Healthcare Recruitment. *Etiquette* has to do with good manners. It's not so much our own good manners, but making other people feel comfortable by the way we behave toward them.

Good ethics and etiquette toward a split placement "partner" is essential in establishing and maintaining a good relationship with another recruiter with whom you are doing split business. These same general principles also apply when working with your clients.

DO's

- Act in good faith at all times. If something does not "feel" right, question it and determine if you should continue.
- Admit to a mistake and take measures to correct it.
- Your share of the work
- Value your split partner's time as well as your own.
- Check your email and messages daily if not hourly. Communicate with your trading partner.
- Be available to your split partner.
- Respect your trading partner and treat that partner in the way you want to be treated.
- Pay your split partner in a timely fashion. When a split partner sends you a candidate, half of any fee collected is already theirs and needs to be paid right away—not when you get around to it.

DON'T

- Be rude, obtrusive, or distrustful.
- Try to hide or ignore a mistake.
- Expect your trading partner to do all the work.
- Email your trading partner with "Call me." Remember your time is no more valuable than your trading partner's time.
- Ignore emails or phone calls.

- Avoid your trading partner.
- Treat your trading partner in a way that is dishonest or disrespectful.

Many Associations such as The Alliance of Medical Recruiters and the National Association of Physician Recruiters have both written and unwritten codes of ethics and behavior. Just remember to treat your trading partner the way you would like to be treated.

Some networks have built in policies that cover split business and do not require an additional agreement with your trading partner. If you do not belong to a network or they do not have policies to cover split partners, you may consider signing an agreement with each partner. An example agreement is below.

Example Split Fee Agreement

Cooperative Placement Split Agreement

1. This Agreement shall establish guidelines equally applicable to the parties participating in this Agreement. Collected fees from cooperative placements shall be split between the firms on a 50/50 basis, including retainer. Placements that involve a third party, or alternate split scenarios, shall be agreed to in writing prior to the placement.

2. The referring party will honor the fee schedule and guarantee period used by firm with the job opening which will be the basis of the split fee agreement between the two firms. If a rebate or a refund has to be made to a client the party referring the candidate will reimburse the firm placing the candidate for their portion of the refund or rebate within 10 days of written notification.

3. This Agreement is binding for a minimum of one (1) year from the date of signing. This Agreement will automatically renew at the end of that twelve-month time period, unless canceled by one of the participating parties to the other in writing. In the event of contract cancellation, any transactions pending must be resolved under the terms listed in this Agreement.

4. The firm making the referral is responsible for providing the current CV and initial interview information for every candidate sent to the receiving firm. They may also be asked to follow-up, check references, or any other actions necessary on the candidate's side in order to make a placement.

5. The firm offering the job opportunity is responsible for the billing and collection of fees from the Client. In the event that a collection becomes 60 days overdue, both parties shall agree in writing on the necessary action and financial commitment required to collect the fee.

6. Any significant action involving a shared applicant or job setting such as an initial interview, second interview, job offer, a rejection, site visit, etc., shall be communicated to the other firm as soon as possible.

7. Payment of split fees shall be made within five (5) working days from the day the payment is received from the Client. A copy of the Client's check, wire transfer statement or other valid evidence of the overall payment from the Client shall be included.

8. The firm offering the job opportunity shall handle all negotiations between the Candidate and Client Company.

9. If the receiving firm has established and can document prior contact from the referred Candidate, they may reject the submittal of that Candidate by phone, mail or email as having 'prior direct' contact with the Candidate. Time limit for this ownership is one (1) year. Information of a candidate on a mailing list, database, job board, etc., does not constitute ownership of a candidate.

10. A Candidate referral remains valid for one (1) years from the date of initial referral. The information provided by the referring firm must include date of referral. Any candidate "in process" at the end of year period shall be considered active and covered by this agreement.

11. Both parties agree that neither agency shall contact the other agency's client directly to collect money owed for a placement or to get a job order on any search where two agencies have actively shared candidates.

12. All candidate information and/or job orders received by either firm will be the property of the referring agency. Candidate and/or job order information shall not be passed along to any 3rd party by the receiving firm without prior approval.

The parties hereto agree that facsimile signatures shall be as effective as the originals.

______________________	______________________
Company Name	Company Name
______________________	______________________
Authorized Representative	Authorized Representative
______________________	______________________
Signature	Signature
______________________	______________________
Title	Title
______________________	______________________
Date	Date

NOTES

NOTES

NOTES

Section Two:

Medical Specialties

Specialty Guide

The following physician specialty sheets are meant to be an introductory guide to for recruiters. They are by no means comprehensive and recruiters should constantly use other resources to research the specialties for which they recruit. It is important to note that most of this information is based in criteria in the United States. Other countries may have requirements and practices that vary from those in the US.

- Training: This can vary per program and may change when new technology requires a candidate to acquire more training. Training is the on-going education they receive post medical school. Training listed is the norm for US Medical Schools. For each specialty, it is implied that they completed medical school.

- Subspecialties: Most specialties have niches that require additional training, usually through a fellowship.

- Abbreviation: These are common abbreviations used by recruiters. These are not universal, but can be useful when documenting or using a database.

Subspecialties: New subspecialties develop as new developments in medicine emerge. Some subspecialties require additional board certification, some require a specialty certificate, and some are "niches" that a physician may have.

Recruitment Tips: This section gives you a few ideas of "need to know" issues that may come up during the recruitment process. The longer you recruit, the more specialty specific information you will learn.

Resources: There are abundant resources on the Internet and most recruiters find it beneficial to research each specialty for which they recruit. Medical technology and requirements for physicians are constantly changing. No client or physician expects a recruiter to be fully knowledgeable of each procedure, but they do expect that you will have a general understanding of each specialty and resources to learn more.

Allergy & Immunology

- Training: Candidate must receive training and certification in Internal Medicine or Pediatrics and additional two years of training (fellowship) in allergy and immunology.
- Subspecialties: None
- Abbreviation: AI

Allergist and Immunologist will treat abnormalities of the body's immune system, particularly with the respiratory system or the skin. The Allergist will treat conditions like allergic rhinitis, sinusitis, asthma, hypersensitivity pneumonitis, occupational lung diseases and other diseases of the respiratory track. He/She will also diagnose and treat reactions to food, drugs, and insect bites.

The Allergist-immunologist will likely order laboratory test that can be used to determine the source of an allergic irritant and how to treat it. He/She may prescribe supplements, drug therapy or simply have the patient avoid the irritant.

Subspecialties: The American Board of Medical Specialties currently does not recognize any *subspecialties* for Allergy and Immunology, however ABMS and American Board of Allergy and Immunology (ABAI) does recognize a duel certification in allergy/immunology and pediatric pulmonology, adult rheumatology, and pediatric rheumatology.

Recruitment Tips: Sometimes these specialists are just called Allergists.

Resources: www.aaaai.org
www.abai.org

Anesthesiology

- Training: 4 Years of training post medical school: one year internship, 3 years residency.
- Subspecialties: Interventional Pain, Sports Medicine
- Abbreviation: AN

Anesthesiology is typically associated with surgery, often referred to as perioperative medicine. The Anesthesiologist is trained to assess patients risk prior to an operation and provide pain relief to patients, during and immediately following an operation, delivery of a baby, or during diagnostic procedures.

The anesthesiologist will plan the appropriate anesthetic for the patient and care for the patient during the surgical procedure. He/She will also monitor the patient's vital signs, adjust the medication, fluids or other factors that provide a safe and pain free procedure.

Subspecialties: A Pain Management Anesthesiologist often works in specialty clinics and treats patients who are experiencing chronic pain problems. He/She may also receive referrals to treat patients with cancer pain. A Palliative care anesthesiologist will provide pain management to patients who are critically ill.

An Anesthesiologist who specializes in Critical Care Medicine will diagnose and treat patients with multiple organ dysfunctions. You will typically find this specialist responsible for intensive care units.

Recruitment Tips: For anesthesiology candidates, it is important to ask if they prefer a traditional anesthesiology practice or position or prefer a pain management practice. Pain management anesthesiologists may not want to take call with a regular anesthesiologist group. Also remember to ask potential candidates if they are comfortable with all scopes of anesthesiology. Some candidates may prefer not to see pediatric, heart, or vascular cases.

In Canada they may be called anaesthetists or anaesthesiologists.

Resources: www.theaba.org

Cardiology

- Training: 3 years if Internal Medicine plus at least 3 years of cardiology training.
- Subspecialties: Non-invasive, Invasive non-interventional, interventional, electrophysiologist
- Abbreviation: CD (Cardiology), CDE (Electrophysiologist), CDINT (Interventional Cardiologist), CDIV (Invasive Cardiologist), CDNO (Non-invasive Cardiology)

Cardiology is one of the more complicated specialties. These specialists treat problems with the heart, arteries, and veins. General cardiologists will manage a patient's cholesterol and triglycerides. They will often treat patients who have had cardiac events. Most of your recruitment needs will require one of the following types of cardiologist:

Non-invasive: These cardiologists will perform evaluations using non-invasive evaluation methods. These include stress echos, transesophageal echos (TEE), and trans thoracic echos (TTE). They also do nuclear studies.

Invasive, Non-interventional: These cardiologists do everything the non-invasive cardiologist does. They also do diagnostic catheterizations.

Interventional: Interventional Cardiologists can do all procedures of the non-invasive and invasive, non-interventional cardiologist. They are the practitioners that surgically fix any blockage by using stents or other methods. They do an extra year of training and take boards in both cardiology and interventional cardiology.

Electrophysiologist: EPs train an extra year and they mainly manage devices such as pacemakers, and defibrillators. They also spend a large portion of their time doing ablations-complex studies of the electro mechanics of how the heart fires.

Recruitment Tips: More so than most specialties, it is very important that you get a clear idea of what kind of cardiologist your client will need. If they aren't sure, they should provide you with list of procedures expected and you may need to do some research on your own.

Resources: www.acc.org
www.aacvpr.org

Critical Care Medicine

- Training: One to two years of fellowship training
- Abbreviation: CCM

Critical Care Medicine is a subspecialty of several other specialties and often a critical component for specific positions. For this reason, a page is dedicated to this subspecialty.

Critical Care Medicine refers to the treatment of patients who are experiencing live threatening conditions. This can include patients who have been in accidents, have terminal conditions, those who have had complications due to surgery or child birth, or even those with respiratory distress. Currently the most common pairings to Critical Care Medicine are Anesthesiology, Internal Medicine, Obstetrics and Gynecology, Pediatrics, and Pulmonology.

You will most frequently find a specialist with training in Critical Care Medicine working in conjunction with the hospital's Intensive Care Unit or sometimes in an Urgent Care clinic. An Anesthesiologist with CCM training will often be utilized in the treatment of patients with multiple organ failure. A Pediatric CCM physician would work with children in the hospitals PICU (pediatric intensive care unit) and the NICU (neonatal intensive care unit).

Recruitment Tips: A Critical Care Medicine physician is often referred to as an "Intensivist" (not to be confused with an "internist", which refers to an Internal Medicine physician) because of working in the Intensive Care Unit. Therefore, a Pediatric CCM physician may be called a "Peds Intensivist" for short.

Because of their work in the ICU, be sure to know the numbers of beds in each ICU department before you contact a candidate. Also find out what kinds of cases they would cover. Depending on the size of the hospital, a CCM Internist may have to cover most ICU cases. In larger hospitals, he/she may only see patients in the general ICU while more specific cases are covered by other specialists (such as Neurologists for a Neuro ICU).

Resources: www.sccm.org
www.pedsccm.org

Colon and Rectal Surgery

- Training: Five years General Surgery Residency plus at least one year Colo-rectal fellowship.
- Abbreviation: CRS

Colon and Rectal Surgery (often called Colo-rectal surgery) is just as it sounds—surgery of the colon and rectum. Colo-rectal surgeons will treat diseases of the colon, rectum, and anus both surgically and non-surgically. They may treat conditions such as hemorrhoids, fissures, tissue infections. They can also perform endoscopic procedures to diagnosis conditions such as cancer or polyps.

Recruitment Tips: This is a highly specialized field and the candidate pool for this kind of search will be very limited. Be sure to know what kinds of cases your client requires of the practitioner. In smaller hospitals or location, the client may also require that a candidate cover general surgery cases or call. In that case, the CRS will need to have maintained his/her board certification and clinical skills for general surgery as well as those for colo-rectal surgery.

Resources: www.abcrs.org
www.fascrs.org

Dermatology

- Training: Four years of residency training
- Subspecialties: Dermatopathology, Pediatric Dermatologist, Clinical and Laboratory Dermatological Immunology
- Abbreviation: D (Dermatology) and DS (Dermatological Surgery)

Dermatologists diagnose and treat conditions of the skin, hair, and sweat glands. They will frequently treat various types of skin cancer and infections of the skin. A Dermatologist will can treat conditions medically or surgically. A Dermatologist who wants to see mostly surgical cases will likely have additional training in Mohs surgical technique. Sometimes a surgical dermatologist will perform cosmetic procedures such as Botox or liposuction.

Subspecialties: A Pediatric Dermatologist will specialize in conditions more commonly found in children, such as birthmarks or hereditary conditions such as Genodermatosis.

A Dermatopathologist will examine and diagnose conditions at a microscopic level.

A Dermatologist who specializes in clinical and laboratory dermatological immunology, referred to as a Immunodermatologist, uses laboratory methods to diagnose immune system disorders.

Recruitment Tips: General Dermatology will be a common search performed by recruiters. Be sure to talk to candidates about their interest and abilities in surgical dermatology as there are some specialists who perform Mohs surgery nearly 100% of the time.

Resources: www.abderm.org

Emergency Medicine

- Training: 3 years or residency training
- Subspecialties: Pediatric Emergency, Medicine, Medical Toxicology, Sports Medicine, Undersea and Hyperbaric Medicine, & Hospice and Palliative Care
- Abbreviation: EM or sometimes ER

Emergency Medicine physicians are the practitioners you will most frequently find in the emergency room. Their training focuses on emergency situations where quick thinking and action could prevent permanent injury or death to patients. They will evaluate, treat, and stabilize patients of all ages. After a patient is out of immediate danger, they will typically prescribe a course of treatment that may include follow-up with other specialist or hospitalization.

Subspecialties: A Pediatric Emergency Medicine physician may be on staff in a emergency room to see all the pediatric patients who require emergency treatment.

A Medical Toxicologist will treat patients who are suspected of being exposed to drugs, chemicals, or radiological agents.

A Sports Medicine specialist in the ER will treat patients who have sports related injuries.

A subspecialist in Undersea and Hyperbaric Medicine will deal with injuries and illness that relate to diving or exposure to hyperbaric chambers.

Hospice and Palliative Care physicians treat patients who are in terminal stages of an illness. They treat a patient's pain while maximizing quality of life.

Recruitment Tips: Most candidates who are seeking Emergency Medicine positions will be residency trained in Emergency Medicine. However, you will frequently find family practitioners or internists who will be interested in Emergency Medicine positions. These candidates cannot be board certified by the American Board of Emergency Medicine. Some clients will consider these candidates, but many require candidates' residency training in emergency medicine.

Resources: www.abem.org

Endocrinology

- Training: 3 years if Internal Medicine plus at least 3 years in an Endocrinology fellowship.
- Subspecialties: Reproductive endocrinology, Pediatric endocrinologist, and Neuroendocrin.
- Abbreviation: END

Endocrinology is a subspecialty of Internal Medicine. Endocrinologists will be treating patients with disorders of the endocrine systems (hormones) frequently treating those with diabetes and metabolic disorders. They frequently utilize laboratory test results to diagnose and to determine a course of treatment.

Subspecialties: A Reproductive Endocrinologist treats patients who have problems with fertility or menstrual function as it pertains to obstetrics.

A Pediatric Endocrinologist will be a Pediatrician who has completed additional training in Endocrinology and will treat juvenile diabetes, variations of physical growth and sexual development, as well as disorders of the endocrine glands.

Although it is unclear if ABMS or ABIM has made this an official subspecialty, the field of Neuroendocrinology was developed to study the endocrine system in interaction with the nervous system.

Recruitment Tips: Be sure to find out if the Endocrinology position will be 100% Endocrinology or will require general Internal Medicine work as well. Rural areas of the country may need someone to do both.

Resources: www.aace.com
www.endo-society.org

Family Practice

- Training: Three years residency training
- Subspecialties: Obstetrics, Geriatrics, Sports Medicine
- Abbreviation: FP, and FP/OB (Family Practice with Obstetrics)

Family Practitioners are medical doctors who provide primary care to patients of all ages. They treat acute and chronic illnesses and provide health education to their patients. They make referrals to other specialists as necessary. Family Practitioners who do Obstetrics see expecting mothers and deliver babies.

A Family Practitioner in a traditional practice will see patients in both clinic and in the hospital. Often you will have Family Practitioners who see all members of the family for much of their life. They may also perform minor surgeries, such as skin lesions, or obstetrics at hospitals where they have privileges. Often, FP's will work in Urgent Care or Outpatient only positions that do not require in-patient follow-up. Many hospitalist programs use FP's as this allows them to cover the in-patient pediatrics that Internists can't cover.

Subspecialties: Family Practitioners who do Obstetrics see expecting mothers and deliver babies. Sometimes an FP will complete a fellowship in Geriatrics in order to see an older patient base. Sometimes these candidates will want to work in conjunction with nursing homes. FP's who complete a fellowship in Sports Medicine will likely want an emphasis on treating sports related injuries.

Recruitment Tips: Make sure to find out if your candidate wants to do obstetrics as part of the practice. Typically FP/OB's will be best suited for smaller areas that do not have OB/GYN's. A Family Practice candidate will also want to know if call duties will include covering the emergency room.

A new trend is for Family Practitioners to work as Hospitalists. Not all clients will consider FP's in a hospitalist role, but it is important to ask as it may increase the number of candidates you can provide them.

Resources: www.aafp.org

Gastroenterology

- Training: 3 years if Internal Medicine plus 2-3 years in a Gastroenterology/Hepatology fellowship.
- Subspecialties: Hepatology
- Abbreviation: GE, however GI is also frequently used.

Gastroenterologists treat disorders of the digestive track including the esophagus, stomach, small intestine, colon and rectum, pancreas, gallbladder, bile ducts and liver. They will treat disorders such as gastroesophageal reflux, hepatitis, peptic ulcer disease, colitis, Irritable Bowel Syndrome, and pancreatitis.

A Gastroenterologist may use diagnostic procedures such as Endoscopic Retrograde Cholangio Pancreatography (ERCP) or Endoscopic Ultrasound (EUS).

Subspecialties: Gastroenterology programs today typically cover Hepatology or Hepatobiliary Medicine which is specifically the study of the liver, pancreas, and the biliary tract.

Recruitment Tips: Always be sure to know if your candidate is able to perform either ERCP's (Endoscopic retrograde cholangiopancreatography) or EUS's (Endoscopic ultrasound). Some Gastroenterologists do both; some don't do either.

Resources: www.acg.gi.org
www.gastro.org

Infectious Disease

- Training: Residency training in Internal Medicine or Pediatric plus two to three years fellowship in Infectious Disease.

- Abbreviation: ID

Infectious Disease physicians specialize in the diagnosis and treatment of infectious diseases. They frequently treat infectious conditions of the sinuses, heart, brain, lungs, urinary tract, bowels, bones, and pelvic organs.

They cover all kinds of infections including those caused by bacteria, viruses, fungi, and parasites. They also see treat patients who are infected with HIV.

An ID physician will review patient histories as well as physically examining the patient.

Subspecialties: Infectious Disease is a practice that is already a subspecialty of either Internal Medicine or Pediatrics. A specialist with residency training in Internal Medicine would see adult patients with infectious disease conditions where as one with residency training in Pediatrics would see children.

You may also see ID specialists with expertise in Travel Medicine and Preventative Medicine.

Recruitment Tips: An Infectious Disease physician will largely receive their referrals from other physicians in the area. Be sure to know how many physicians may refer to them as well as the service area that would cover.

Resources: www.idsociety.org

Internal Medicine

- Training: Three years residency training
- Subspecialties: See full list below
- Abbreviation: IM

Internal Medicine physicians are primary care physicians for adults. They are referred to as Internists. General internists will see patients in an office treating chronic and acute illnesses. They may see the same patients for many years. You also find Internists who work in the hospital and see patients for other practitioners. These are called Hospitalists.

Subspecialties: Internal Medicine is the stepping stone for many specialties (most of which have been covered in these specialty pages). Most specialists will become boarded in Internal Medicine as well as take an additional exam to become boarded in their specialty. The length of fellowship training varies for each specialty.

These are the specialties where an Internist can complete additional training: Adolescent Medicine, Cardiovascular Disease, Clinical Cardiac Electrophysiology, Critical Care Medicine, Endocrinology (Diabetes and Metabolism), Gastroenterology, Geriatric Medicine, Hematology, Hospice and Palliative Medicine, Infectious Disease, Interventional Cardiology, Medical Oncology, Nephrology, Pulmonary Disease, Rheumatology, Sleep Medicine, Sports Medicine, and Transplant Hepatology.

Recruitment Tips: This is one of the most common and most diverse specialties. Often Internists may have a "niche" in areas that are typically subspecialties. For example they may do a lot of gastroenterology procedures and therefore may be able to see a wider patient base.

Besides traditional Internal Medicine clinics and outpatient clinics, one of the most common positions for an Internist is as a Hospitalist. For that reason is it critical to find out what kind of positions they want to explore. For Hospitalist positions, it is important to find out what kind of scheduling they use (i.e. 7 days on/7 days off). They will also want to know more information about the size of the hospital, level of trauma, and ICU care since they will often be responsible for these patients.

Resources: www.abim.org
www.acponline.org

Internal Medicine/Pediatrics

- Training: Minimum of 4 years residency training
- Abbreviation: IMP

Physicians who have completed a combined Internal Medicine and Pediatrics program are often referred to as Med-Peds. They are similar to Family Practitioners as they can see all age ranges, but the structure and philosophies of their training and practice are different. Their training covers the full scope of both Internal Medicine and Pediatrics so they typically become board certified in both areas. There is no board specifically for Med-Peds.

Med-Peds can work in a clinic seeing patients with routine health issues or they may choose to work as Hospitalist.

Subspecialties: With the unique nature of this program, it gives great flexibility for residents to enter a fellowship training program. They can apply for fellowship programs in all of the same subspecialties that Internists or Pediatricians may pursue. It would put them in the position of being able to see all ages of the given subspecialty.

Recruitment Tips: Med-Peds have been one of the more highly sought after specialties in recent years. Much of that has to do with their flexibility in practice. Many clients seek them for Hospitalist positions.

Be sure your Med-Ped candidate is or plans to become board certified in both Pediatrics and Internal Medicine.

Resources: www.medpeds.org
www.aap.org/sections/med-peds/101.htm

Neonatal-Perinatal Medicine

- Training: Neonatologists require three years of Pediatrics plus 2-3 additional years training in a Neonatal fellowship. Perinatologists are the same as Maternal-Fetal Medicine specialists. Their residency training is in Obstetrics and Gynecology with a fellowship in Perinatal Medicine.
- Abbreviation: NPM

Neonatal relates to a newborn in the first month after birth. Perinatal refers to the period approximately 22 weeks into a pregnancy and a short period of time after the pregnancy. From this information one can deduce that a Neonatologist and a Perinatologist are physicians who treat the fetus before delivery and an infant immediately after delivery. Their care is often required if a baby is considered high-risk due to the mother's condition (i.e. multiple miscarriages, entopic pregnancies) or identified health problems with the fetus.) They are often utilized in cases of multiple births. Although Neonatology and Perinatology overlap, ideally a Perinatologist would care for a fetus before birth and a Neonatologist would care for an infant immediately after birth.

Additional Subspecialty information: Neonatology is a subspecialty of Pediatrics. Perinatology is a subspecialty of Obstetrics and the specialists are often referred to as Obstetricians since the field of study overlaps. They may also be referred to as Maternal-Fetal Medicine physicians.

Recruitment Tips: This is a highly specialized field and you will primarily find practice opportunities in suburban to metro sized areas. For the Perinatologist, find out from your client how much clinical work versus consulting will be required. You may also need to find out if the position will require that they cover general obstetrics.

Resources: www.nationalperinatal.org
www.neonatology.org

Nephrology

- Training: 3 years if Internal Medicine plus at least two years of a nephrology fellowship.
- Subspecialties: Pediatric nephrology
- Abbreviation: NEP

Nephrologists treat and diagnose conditions of the kidneys including their function and disease. This may include treatment of electrolyte disturbances and hypertension. They may care for patients who need renal replacement therapy, dialysis, and renal transplants. Sometimes Nephrologists may treat autoimmune diseases or lupus as well.

Subspecialties: Pediatric Nephrology focuses on the same conditions above as found in pediatric patients.

Although not typically classified as subspecialty, some Nephrologists may go through additional training to be certified as Interventional Nephrologists. They would be able to perform procedures such as insertion of tunneled hemodialysis and peritoneal dialysis catheters, endovascular procedures, and diagnostic sonography.

Recruitment Tips: As with most subspecialties of Internal Medicine, find out when recruiting for Nephrology if the position will require any General Internal Medicine work.

Resources: www.asn-online.org
www.asdin.org

Neurological Surgery

- Training: At least 6 years of training (usually 7) which includes surgical training
- Abbreviation: NS

Neurosurgeons are trained to treat conditions of the brain, such as brain tumors, brain trauma, and blood vessel disorders both surgical and nonsurgical . They also perform spine surgery. They focus on treatment of the central, peripheral and autonomic nervous system. They will also treat pain both surgically and non-surgically.

Subspecialties: There are subcategories of Neurosurgery, although not officially subspecialties. All require at least one year of additional training. Those include Pediatric Neurosurgery, Endovascular Neurosurgery, Interventional Neuroradiology, Neuro-Oncology, Spine, Skull Base Surgery, and Epilepsy Surgery. As this ever developing field, new fields of study emerge regularly.

Recruitment Tips: Neurosurgeons are one of the more difficult specialties to recruit. Plan to have excellent data about the opportunity to present. Neurosurgery candidates may want to know if a gamma knife is available at your facility. They may also want to know how many neuro-ICU beds are available. When a client is looking for a Spine Surgeon, find out what kind of training they require. They may require a Neurosurgeon, but they may also consider Orthopedic Surgeons who can cover spine cases.

Resources: www.aans.org
www.abns.org

Neurology

- Training: Residency in neurology, typically 4 years
- Subspecialties: Vascular Neurology, Pain Medicine, Neuromuscular Medicine, Neurodevelopmental Disabilities, Hospice and Palliative Medicine, & Clinical Neurophysiology
- Abbreviation: N

Neurologists treat and diagnosis conditions of the brain such as epilepsy, brain tumors, strokes, dementia, or even headaches. They also treat conditions of the spinal cord and peripheral nerves. They may employ electroencephalography (EEG) or electromyography (EMG) to diagnosis conditions.

Subspecialties: A Neurologist may specialize in Sleep Medicine and treat patients with sleep disorders. These candidates will want information about the hospital's sleep lab. A Vascular Neurologist treats vascular diseases of the nervous system.

A Neurologist with special training in Pain Medicine or Hospice and Palliative Medicine may treat patients with chronic pain related to cancer of other neurological conditions.

A Neurologist may also specialize in diagnosing and treating disorders of the nerve, muscle, or neuromuscular junction. These specialists require additional training in Neuromuscular Medicine.

A specialist in Neurodevelopmental Disabilities may diagnose and treat patients with cerebral palsy, mental retardation or chronic behavioral conditions.

Physicians with additional training in Clinical Neurophysiology will manage central, peripheral and autonomic nervous system disorders.

Recruitment Tips: Neurology has some overlap with Neurosurgery and Psychiatry. Be sure to ask clients what procedures candidates will be expected to do. Since this specialty has a wide variety of subspecialty possibilities, find out what kind of training your client requires.

Resources: www.ninds.nih.gov
www.abpn.com

Nuclear Medicine

- Training: Minimum of 3 years residency training in nuclear medicine
- Abbreviation: NM

Nuclear Medicine is a specialized area of Radiology. Nuclear Medicine physicians use radioactive substances, called radionuclides or tracers, to create images of the body and its organs. They use this data to evaluate molecular, metabolic, physiologic, or pathologic conditions of the body. They use PET or CT scans in conjunction with anatomic imagining. These interventions are useful in detecting cancer as well monitoring the effects of treatment. They can diagnose many kinds of diseases and determine if organs in the body are functioning normally.

These specialists are usually referred to by other physicians. They have limited involvement in patient care. Their work often requires a large degree of research.

Subspecialties: You may find physicians who have completed combined programs in Internal Medicine or studied Radiology as well.

Recruitment Tips: This is an ever changing field. It is important to ask a client which procedures they will need the candidate to do. You will typically find a Nuclear Medicine physician working in a hospital or university hospital.

Resources: www.abnm.org
www.snm.org

Obstetrics & Gynecology

- Training: Four years residency training on Obstetrics and Gynecology
- Subspecialties: Critical Care Medicine, Gynecological Oncology, Maternal-Fetal Medicine, Reproductive Endocrinology
- Abbreviation: OBG or OB/GYN. GYNON (Gynecology Oncology), OBS (Obstetrics), OBGHOSP (OB/GYN Hospitalist), GYN (Gynecology)

An OB/GYN is the physician who cares for a women's overall reproductive care. Obstetrics refers to the care of a female patient before and immediately after pregnancy. Gynecology refers to practices required to maintain the health of a women's reproductive system. Both of these practices require both surgical and non-surgical skills.

Subspecialties: A Maternal-Fetal Medicine specialist will see patients who are high-risk due to the conditions of the mother (i.e. history of miscarriages) or issues with the fetus. This specialty is the same is a Perinatal physician.

An OB/GYN who specializes in Critical Care Medicine may work in conjunction with a hospitals ICU.

A Gynecological Oncologist will treat patients with gynecological cancers such ovarian cancer.

A Reproductive Endocrinology treats patients who are seeking treatment for infertility.

Recruitment Tips: It is important to note that OB/GYNs can take their written boards upon completion of their residency program, but they must wait to take their oral examinations until they have "collected" enough cases. This often takes two years post-residency.

Sometimes clients may also use FP/OB's and midwives. Be sure your OB/GYN candidate is comfortable working with both. Also, in most OB/GYN's do an even mix of Obstetrics and Gynecology, but in some instances, they may choose to practice only one.

Resources: www.abog.org
www.acog.org

Oncology

- Training: 3 years if Internal Medicine plus at least 3 year training specific to Oncology
- Subspecialties: Hematology/Oncology, Gynecology/Oncology, & Radiation/Oncology, Surgical oncology
- Abbreviation: HO (Hematology/Oncology), GSON (Surgical oncologist), GYNON (Gynecology/Oncology), MO (Medical Oncology), PHO (Pediatric Hematology/Oncology), RO (Radiation Oncology

Oncology specialties are all subspecialties of Internal Medicine. This sheet was provided to assist recruitment professionals in further the distinction between Oncologists.

Oncologists are specialists who care for an individual who has cancer. They will be involved in their diagnosis, treatment and pain management. A General Oncologist is referred to as a Medical Oncologist.

Subspecialties: A Hematologist/Oncologist is a specialist who treats diseases of cancer of the blood. A Pediatric Hematologist/Oncologist will complete 3 years of a pediatric residency and 3 years of training in Hematology/Oncology.

A Gynecologist/Oncologist will treat patients with gynecological cancer both through surgery and medicinal treatment.

A Radiation Oncologist uses radiation therapy to treat patients with cancer.

A Surgical Oncologist specializes in tumor removal.

Recruitment Tips: Although you still find many practicing Medical Oncologists, it is becoming ever prevalent for medical oncologists to also be Hematologist/Oncologists. Clients will often ask that they are "triple boarded"- meaning boarded in Internal Medicine, Medical Oncology, and Hematology Oncology.

Resources: www.asco.org

Ophthalmology

- Training: 4 to 5 years residency training in ophthalmology
- Abbreviation: OPH

Ophthalmologists are practitioners who diagnosis and treat conditions of the eye and conditions affecting the visual pathway. They may consult with other optic specialists in managing conditions such as diabetes, hypertension, and ocular inflammation. An Ophthalmologist can also prescribe vision services such as glass or contact lenses.

Subspecialties: The ABMS does not officially recognize any subspecialties for Ophthalmology. However, the American Academy of Ophthalmology recognizes several areas where Ophthalmologists may be further specialized through additional training. These include Cornea and External Disease, Cataract and Refractive Surgery, Glaucoma, Uveitis and Ocular Immunology, Vitreoretinal Diseases, Ophthalmic Plastic Surgery, Pediatric Ophthalmology, Neuro-ophthalmology, and Ophthalmic Pathology.

Recruitment Tips: Note that although Ophthalmologists and Optometrists treat very similar conditions of the eye, they are not the same. The primary difference is that an Ophthalmologist is a surgeon. They are both highly educated, but Optometrists are not medical doctors. They attend a training program much like dentists.

As noted above, there are several areas where an Ophthalmologist can have a degree of specialization. Be sure to ask your client more about their training requirements.

Resources: www.aao.org
www.abop.org

Orthopedic Surgery

- Training: Minimum of 5 years residency training
- Subspecialties: Sports Medicine, Hand, Foot and Ankle, Spine, Adult Reconstructive Surgery/Total Joints, Pediatrics, Trauma
- Abbreviation: ORS (Subspecialties will include ORS as part of abbreviation)

[Orthopedics is also often spelled "Orthopaedics"] An Orthopedist is a specialist who treats conditions or injuries of the musculoskeletal system through surgery, medicinal means, or potentially physical manipulation. Surgical interventions can include repair or replacement of structures such as the hips, knees, or other joints.

Subspecialties: The two subspecialties that have certificates are Sports Medicine and Hand Orthopedics. Sports Medicine Orthopedic Surgeons will treat patients who have athletic related injuries. A Hand Specialist will treat conditions of the hand and wrist.

There are several other areas where an Orthopedic Surgeon can sub-specialize. Most are self explanatory and include Foot and Ankle, Spine, Pediatrics, and Trauma. A specialist who does Total Joint Reconstruction (also called Adult Reconstructive Surgery) may repair or replace knees, hips, shoulders and will facilitate follow-up rehabilitation.

Recruitment Tips: In the case of each subspecialty, you may also find General Surgeons who have completed additional training in these areas. Some clients will consider these candidates, but often won't because they may require the candidate to cover call for General Orthopedics (which a General Surgeon couldn't do).

As with other surgical specialties, Orthopedic Surgeons can take their written boarding exams immediately after training. However this process isn't complete until they have "collected" enough surgical cases to take the oral boards. This normally takes two years.

Be sure to ask your client what kind of cases they expect an Orthopedic Surgeon to cover. A frequent issue is if they can cover spine cases. Also be sure to find out if an Orthopedic Surgeon will be required to cover General Surgery call and what mix of specialty cases versus general orthopedics than can expect. For an Orthopedic Specialist, find out how much general orthopedics they can expect.

Resources: www.aaos.org
www.abos.org

Otolaryngology

- Training: Minimum of 5 years residency training
- Subspecialties: Neurotology, Pediatric Otolaryngology, Plastic Surgery Within the Head and Neck & Sleep Medicine
- Abbreviation: OTO (although you may often see ENT)

Otolaryngologists are also called ENT's—Ear, Nose and Throat physicians. You'll also see this specialty listed as Otorhinolaryngologists. *Oto* refers to ears, *Rhino* refers to the nose, and *Laryngo* refers to throat. They treat patients both medicinally and surgically. As the name implies, they treat all conditions of the ear, nose, and throat and related conditions of the head and neck.

Subspecialties: There are four subspecialty certificates for Otolaryngology.

A physician specializing in Neurotology treats diseases and conditions of the ear and temporal bone. This includes issues with hearing and balance.

A Pediatric Otolaryngologist sees infants and children, often treats childhood disorders related to hearing, language, and speech.

An Otolaryngologist may specialize in Plastic Surgery within the Head and Neck. This specialist may perform surgery to correct issues from birth (such as a cleft pallet) or oncology cases as well as cosmetic.

Sleep Medicine Otolaryngologists would assess and treat conditions that interfere with the sleep cycle. The will use a sleep laboratory to diagnosis the issue and determine a course of treatment.

Recruitment Tips: Find out from your clients what kinds of cases your candidate will need to see. They may require just a general OTO or they may require someone who does more specialty work.

Resources: www.aboto.org
www.entnet.org

Hospice and Palliative Medicine

- Training: One to two years of fellowship training after residency training in field of specialty
- Abbreviation: PLM

Hospice is the concept of care that is provided to patients who are terminally ill and no longer responding to treatment. This form of care is not-intended to prolong their lives. Palliative Medicine is the practice of caring for patients through symptom and pain management. The goal of physicians practicing Hospice and Palliative care is to improve quality of life for patients in the last days of their lives. They may work in a hospital, in conjunction with nursing homes, or even visit patients in their home where other Hospice providers are already in place.

Although these are frequently paired together, these specialists may also practice Palliative Care in non-hospice situations. They may be working in conjunction with other physicians who are using treatments to cure a patient's condition.

Subspecialties: Hospice and Palliative Care is actually a subspecialty of several other specialties. In 2008, a subspecialty certificate became available for physicians who have completed additional training in Palliative Medicine and taken a written examination.

These are the areas of medicine that allow subspecialty certificates in Hospice and Palliative: Anesthesiology, Emergency Medicine, Family Medicine, Internal Medicine, Pediatrics, Physical Medicine and Rehabilitation, Psychiatry, Neurology, Radiology, Surgery, Vascular Surgery,

Recruitment Tips: When a client needs a Palliative Medicine physician, find out what kind of residency training they would accept.

Resources: www.nhpco.org
www.aahpm.org

Pathology

- Training: 3 or 4 years of residency training
- Subspecialties: Blood Banking/Transfusion Medicine, Chemical Pathology, Cytopathology, Dermatopathology, Forensic Pathology, Hematology, Medical Microbiology, Molecular Genetic Pathology, Neuropathology, Pediatric Pathology
- Abbreviation: CLP (Clinical Pathology), ATP (Anatomic Pathology), PTH (Anatomic/Clinical Pathology)

Pathology is often simply referred to as the study of disease. These physicians examine samples of tissue, fluid, or organs typically through laboratory processes. Medical Pathologists are divided into Clinical and Anatomic Pathologists. When they do both they are considered General Pathologists.

An Anatomic Pathologist would perform autopsies and does not see patients, but study tissue at the molecular level. A Clinical Pathologist will study fluids using a variety of tools.

Subspecialties: Subspecialty certificates are available in the following fields: Blood Banking/Transfusion Medicine, Chemical Pathology, Cytopathology, Dermatopathology, Forensic Pathology, Hematology, Medical Microbiology, Molecular Genetic Pathology, Neuropathology, Pediatric Pathology. For more detailed information on Pathology subspecialties: www.abms.org/Who_We_Help/Consumers/About_Physician_Specialties/pathology.aspx

Recruitment Tips: Generally when you have a Pathology candidate, he/she will be a General Pathologist, but always be sure to ask the candidate if there is a niche or special practice interest. Pathology is a specialty that you may only recruit for once in a while.

Resources: www.abpath.org
www.ascp.org

Pediatrics

- Training: At least three years residency training
- Subspecialties: See below
- Abbreviation: PD or sometimes PED

Pediatricians provide routine and acute care for children. They may see an individual from infancy through adolescence. Besides treating issues that are also common to adults, a Pediatrician will treat conditions related to growth and development. Pediatricians also have the unique situation of treating a child who is under a parent's care; therefore they must take into consideration legal as well coordinating care.

Subspecialties: Nearly every specialty that focuses on the care for adults has a pediatric counterpart. A Pediatric Subspecialist will complete residency training in Pediatrics then fellowship training in the area of specialty (such as Pediatric Gastroenterology or Pediatric Cardiology).

There are some subspecialties unique to Pediatrics:

Child Abuse Pediatrics, Developmental-Pediatrics, Neonatology.

Recruitment Tips: A commonly asked question by Pediatric candidates: Are required to attend deliveries? They may also want to know if they will be doing circumcisions.

Resources: www.aap.org
www.abp.org

Plastic Surgery

- Training: Five to seven years residency training in Plastic Surgery
- Subspecialties: Head and Neck; Hand Surgery
- Abbreviation: PS

Plastic Surgeons primarily use surgical methods to alter a patient's physical appearance. They operate to repair or reconstruct tissue or the musculoskeletal system. A patient may elect to have procedures performed such as breast or nose reconstruction. Those procedures are primarily considered cosmetic procedures since they are to alter what is otherwise already normal. If a surgery is required to restore the appearance due to a trauma, physical deformity, infection, tumor, or disease, these are considered reconstructive procedures.

Subspecialties: A subspecialty certificate is available for two subspecialties. Those are Plastic Surgery within the Head and Neck and Surgery of the Hand.

There are several other areas where a Plastic Surgeon may receive additional training and specialization. Those include Craniofacial Surgery, Microsurgery, Pediatrics, Burn Surgery, and Facial Plastics and Reconstruction.

Recruitment Tips: It is important to find out from your client the mix of cosmetic procedures to reconstructive procedures. A physician who does mostly cosmetic procedures may prefer a private practice, but be sure to ask the candidate what types of positions are of interest.

It will also be important to find out a candidate's willingness and capability to cover pediatrics cases.

Resources: www.abplsurg.org
www.plasticsurgery.org

Physical Medicine and Rehabilitation

- Training: 4 years of training post medical school. 1 year internship and 3 years residency
- Subspecialties: Interventional Pain Management, Hospice and Palliative Medicine, Neuromuscular Medicine, Spinal Cord Injury, Pediatric Physical Medicine
- Abbreviation: PM

Physical Medicine and Rehab is often referred to as Rehabilitative Medicine. Physiatrists (fiz-eye-a-trists), as they are called, treat acute and chronic pain and musculoskeletal disorders. They treat conditions ranging from sore shoulders and strained ankles to serious spinal cord injuries. Physiatrists may treat patients with sports related injuries or patients with labor or repetition related pain such as lower back pain or carpel tunnel. They will perform a complete history and physical to determine the source of the pain and the best course of treatment. They may use electrodiagnostics to evaluate muscle and nerve damage.

After determining the specific cause for pain, a Physiatrist may direct a treatment team of physical therapist, athletic trainers, or other medical professionals.

Subspecialties: A Physiatrist may work in a hospice environment and treat pain in patients who have terminal medical issues. A Physiatrist who sees pediatrics patients may treat cerebral palsy or spina bifida. A Physiatrist who specializes in Interventional Pain will use injections and other treatments and often work in a pain clinic.

Recruitment Tips: Make sure what type of practice is of interest.

Resources: www.abpmr.org

Preventative Medicine

- Training: Three years residency training
- Subspecialties: Aerospace Medicine and Occupational Medicine
- Abbreviation: PRVM

As the name implies, Preventative Medicine is a specialty that focuses on the overall health of individuals and the general population by promoting practices to prevent disease, disability or death. This specialty often intersects with public health. These practitioners may be involved in community practices such as health inspections of public water and pools, inspection of places that prepare and serve food, and even inspection of industrial situations.

The general practice of Preventative Medicine will include the study of communities and populations, behavioral sciences, and occupational medicine. They may work with individual patients or large populations.

Subspecialties: There are two subspecialty certificates for Preventative Medicine. A Medical Toxicology Specialist is most commonly found working in academics or governmental settings. He/She may deal with issues such poisoning, drug addiction, or hazardous materials. A specialist in Undersea and Hyperbaric Medicine commonly treats decompression illnesses or injuries related to diving accidents.

You may also find Preventative Medicine physicians with niches in Aerospace Medicine or Occupational Medicine.

Recruitment Tips: Preventative Medicine is a specialty that is rarely asked for by clients. However, if they do, you will want to be sure to ask what kind of function they will serve.

Resources: www.abprevmed.org
www.acpm.org/apmr.htm

Psychiatry

- Training: Four years residency training
- Subspecialties: Child/Adolescent Psychiatry, Addiction Psychiatry, Forensic Psychiatry, Geriatric psychiatry, Clinical Neurophysiology, Hospice and Palliative Care, Pain Medicine, Psychosomatic Medicine, and Sleep Medicine
- Abbreviations: P (Psychiatry), CHP (Child/Adolescent Psychiatry), ADP (Addiction Psychiatry), PFP (Forensic Psychiatry), PYG (Geriatric Psychiatry)

Psychiatrists specialize in the diagnosis and treatment of individuals with mental, emotional, or addictive disorders. They may see patients in their office where they would use a variety of talk therapy techniques to diagnose an issue. This may also include a complete review of personal and medical history. In some cases, they may order neuroimages to see if physical conditions of the brain are the cause of a patient's condition. A Psychiatrist may also see patients in an in-patient setting, such as the psychiatry unit of a hospital or a hospital specializing in mental health. A Psychiatrist may use therapeutic techniques such as hypnosis, medicinal interventions, or even physical interventions such as electoconvulsion therapy.

Subspecialties: There are several areas of Psychiatry where additional training and certification is available. Addiction Psychiatry focuses on individuals with alcohol and substance abuse. Child/Adolescent Psychiatry focuses on issues related to children whereas a Geriatric Psychiatrist specializes in conditions related to aging. A Psychiatrist with training in Clinical Neurophysiology may use EEGs or EMGs to help diagnose a condition.

A Psychiatrist who has training in Hospice and Palliative Care will work with the hospice team to assist with the psychological needs of the patient and family. Those with expertise in Psychosomatic Medicine treat patients who have psychological conditions related to medical conditions.

Recruitment Tips: A Psychiatrist is often confused with a Psychologist, who is not a medical doctor. A Psychologist may also have therapeutic sessions, but in most US locations, cannot prescribe medication (although this has recently been under debate).

The age of patients is a common issue when recruiting for Psychiatry. Find out if your candidate will need to see both adults and adolescent patients.

Resources: www.abpn.com
www.psych.org

Pulmonology/Pulmonary Disease

- Training: 3 years residency in Internal Medicine and at least 2 years training in Pulmonary Disease (Note: Most Pulmonology Specialists have completed separate or combined programs that also cover Critical Care Medicine)

- Abbreviation: PUD (Pulmonology), PDP (Pediatric Pulmonology)

A Pulmonologist is a physician who treats diseases of the lungs and the airway. This includes conditions such as bronchitis, asthma, pneumonia and sleep disorders. Since pulmonology deals with the respiratory track and a patient's ability to breathe, they typically have additional training in critical care medicine.

Pulmonologists will primarily diagnose and treat patients through examination, histories, and laboratory evaluation. They often use medicinal interventions as well as oxygen therapy. They may work closely with Cardiothoracic Surgeons in order to fully treat a patient's pulmonary condition.

Subspecialties: Pulmonology is classified as a subspecialty of Internal Medicine. A Pulmonologist who sees pediatric patients will have completed a Pediatric residency and then additional training in Pulmonology. Some Pulmonologists also do Sleep Medicine.

Recruitment Tips: Normally a Pulmonology candidate will become triple boarded: Internal Medicine, Pulmonology, and Critical Care Medicine. Your client may also require this.

Be sure to find out from your client how much work will be done in the office versus the hospital ICU.

Resources: www.aabronchology.org
www.chestnet.org

Radiology

- Training: Five years of residency training (also may vary within the various disciplines)
- Subspecialties: See notes below
- Abbreviation: R (General Radiology)

A Radiologist uses imaging technology to diagnose and treat patients. A Radiologist is most commonly known to use x-rays, but may also use a wide variety and ever growing number of other methodologies such as PET scans, CTs, and ultrasounds to name a few.

Subspecialties: Radiology is divided into three disciplines: Diagnostic Radiology, Radiation Oncology, and Radiological Physics. Each discipline has its own subspecialties. In general, a recruiter will focus on Diagnostic Radiology and Radiation Oncology.

Diagnostic Radiology includes Neuroradiology, Nuclear Radiology, Pediatric Radiology, Vascular and Interventional Radiology, and Hospice and Palliative Medicine.

Radiation Oncology deals with the treatment of cancer and related conditions through use of radiant energy. Hospice and Palliative Medicine is a subspecialty of Radiation Oncology and focuses on the treatment of patients with life-limiting cancer.

Recruitment Tips: Radiology searches often need a General Radiologist, but they may require candidates who have interventional skills.

Teleradiology has become a popular dynamic in recruitment. This is when images are electronically sent to an off-site location for interpretation by a Radiologist. This allows some Radiologist to work from home, or even in another city.

Resources: www.theabr.org
www.acr.org

Rheumatology

- Training: 3 years if Internal Medicine plus at least two years of a rheumatology fellowship.
- Subspecialties: Pediatric Rheumatology
- Abbreviation: RHU

A Rheumatologists is best known for the treatment of rheumatoid arthritis and issues with joints and soft connective tissue. They also treat conditions such as lupus, scleroderma, and other systemic, inflammatory, autoimmune diseases. A Rheumatologist is often consulted when a patient's pain can't be diagnosed. In some cases, a Rheumatologist would see who have muscle strain related to sports injuries.

Subspecialties: A Pediatric Rheumatologist would complete a residency in Pediatrics instead of Internal Medicine.

Recruitment Tips: Rheumatology is a heavily researched field and candidates may want the opportunity to be involved in academic work or research. A Rheumatologist may desire to do some Internal Medicine work combined with Rheumatology in order to have a largely clinical practice. Some Rheumatologist will want more consulting work.

Resources: www.rheumatology.org

Surgery (General and others uncovered)

- Training: Five years residency training
- Subspecialties: Hospice and Palliative Medicine, Pediatric Surgery, Surgery of the Hand, Surgical Critical Care
- Abbreviation: GS (General Surgery)

The foundation for all surgical specialties is General Surgery. A General Surgeon focuses on surgical intervention to the abdominal organs or torso. Common surgeries include appendectomies, hernias, breast tumors, and bowel obstructions. You'll find General Surgeons in almost any population. The depth of surgeries they perform may depend on the availability of other surgical specialist in the area.

Subspecialties: Subspecialty certificates are available for a surgeon in these areas: Hospice and Palliative Medicine, Pediatric Surgery, Surgery of the Hand, Surgical Critical Care. A General Surgeon may also choose to do additional fellowship training and specialize in Trauma, Breast Surgery, Transplant Surgery, or other surgical specialties noted in the specialty guide.

Recruitment Tips: As with any surgical specialty, research the location of the operating room they will be using and any OR amenities that are available. Because of continual advances in medicine and surgical interventions, surgical subspecialties are likely to stay very dynamic. Recruiters will need to keep themselves up-to-date on changes in training and certification for surgeons.

Always be sure to find out what kind of surgeries your candidate will be asked to perform. Surgeons asking for a "bread and butter" position will typically only want basic procedures such as appendicitis, gall bladder removal, and other common surgeries. They may ask not to do breast, trauma, or critical care surgery.

Resources: home.absurgery.org

Thoracic Surgery

- Training: Six to eight years of residency training
- Subspecialties: Cardiothoracic Surgery
- Abbreviation: TS (Thoracic), CTS (Cardiothoracic)

Thoracic Surgery involves surgical treatment to the thorax or otherwise called the chest. This includes the tissue in the chest, lungs & esophagus (among others areas). Thoracic Surgeons must have a thorough knowledge of the respiratory system as well as heart function. If a physician is strictly a Thoracic Surgeon, he/she will not perform cardiac cases.

Subspecialties: A Cardiothoracic Surgeon (which what is more commonly found) is a Surgeon who can perform surgery on all areas of the chest, including the heart.

Recruitment Tips: This specialty seems to be on the decline due to developments in medicine and surgical procedures. Although you still find Thoracic and Cardiothoracic surgeons, some clients cover cardiac cases through Vascular/Endovascular Surgeons and Cardiac Specialists. Be sure to find out what kinds of procedures are required so you know if your candidate is a fit.

Some older Cardiothoracic Surgeons have done additional training so they can meet the requirement of covering vascular/endovascular cases. A Cardiothoracic Surgeon also may not want to take a General Thoracic position but will need to perform a number of cardiac surgeries per year to stay certified.

Resources: www.abts.org
www.aats.org
www.ctsnet.org

Urology

- Training: Five years of residency training, including at least one year dedicated to general surgery.
- Subspecialties: Pediatric Urology
- Abbreviation: U

An Urologist is a specialist who diagnoses and treats diseases of the urinary track and reproductive organs. Although treatment requires assessment through clinical means, surgery is a large component of this specialty. An Urologist will treat disorders such as incontinence, cancer, erectile dysfunction, and infertility in both male and female patients.

Subspecialties: Pediatric Urology focuses on the urological health of pediatric patients and may obtain a subspecialty certificate. A Pediatric Urologist may be more likely to treat younger patients with congenital abnormalities. The American Urological Association had identified other subspecialties as well. These include Urologic Oncology, Renal Transplantation, Male Infertility, Calculi (urinary track stones), Female Urology, and Neurourology.

Recruitment Tips: It is important to find out from candidates if they specialize in any particular area of Urology. For example, some female Urologists may specialize in treating female patients, but not necessarily. For this reason, it is also important that you find out from clients if their Urology position is for a General Urologist or if they need someone with an area of specialization.

Since minimally invasive surgery techniques are largely used in Urology, it is important to know if your practitioner is trained to use the Da Vinci Robot Surgical System, or simply the Da Vinci Robot. A Urology candidate will likely also want to know if the Da Vinci is available in the operating room.

Resources: www.auanet.org
www.abu.org

Vascular Surgery

- Training: Five to six years residency training
- Abbreviation: VS

Vascular Surgery is a subspecialty of General Surgery. They specialize in using surgical interventions to treat conditions of the arteries, veins, and lymphatic systems, although they are also trained in non-surgical interventions as well. They may be utilized with patients who have had a stroke or blockage of the arteries. The conditions treated by a Vascular Surgeon used to be commonly covered by General and Cardiac Surgeons. However emerging science and technology has put the demand for surgeons to specialize further their training in Vascular Surgery. A Vascular Surgeon has a strong General Surgery background and depending on the program, at least two years in General Surgery alone.

A Vascular Surgeon with recent training is likely to have the most up-to-date skills in minimally invasive surgical techniques. This is referred to as Endovascular Surgery and sometimes requires an additional fellowship. These procedures include balloon angioplasties and stents.

Recruitment Tips: Clients with Vascular Surgery positions may require specific training in Vascular or Endovascular Surgery. However sometimes they will accept a General Surgeon who has had recent training to include vascular techniques. Sometimes Cardiothoracic Surgeons have vascular surgery skills, but may not always meet the client's specific educational requirements. Be sure to ask Vascular Surgery candidates if they will do General Surgery as well as Vascular Surgery. They may be required to cover General Surgery call, but not do General Surgery on a routine basis. A need to perform or cover General Surgery will likely require that the Vascular Surgeon maintain board certification in both General and Vascular Surgery.

Resources: www.vascularweb.org

NOTES

Section Three:
Paperless Office

LESSON ONE: BECOME A LEAN, MEAN, PAPERLESS MACHINE

Let us step into a paperless world. It is not a step just to feel ultra-techy or cool. This step is the most efficient and safe way to conduct your everyday business and personal operations. A nice side effect is that you will be completely organized. One note to remember: This section is designed for the PC user. **Instructions may vary depending on your version of Windows.**

Your first step is to create storage for all your documents instead of your bulging file cabinets that you have sworn for the past few years to clean out. Your storage will be on your computer's hard drive. You begin by creating folders for every category of document you can think of. My folders include resumes, invoices, Web Hosting Invoices, Holding, Calls (yes, I even call clients from one of these folders with no paper), Candidate Interviews, Paid Invoices, Policy replies, etc.

You can make folders for personal addresses, birthdays, special events, etc. Anyway, you get the picture. List every type of document you receive and create a folder for that type.

Think of these folders as files in your filing cabinet. You will eventually replace most of your "paper" files with your computer "file cabinet."

To create a new folder on your computer, complete the following steps:

1) Double-click "My Computer" from your Windows screen. It will be an icon of a little computer.

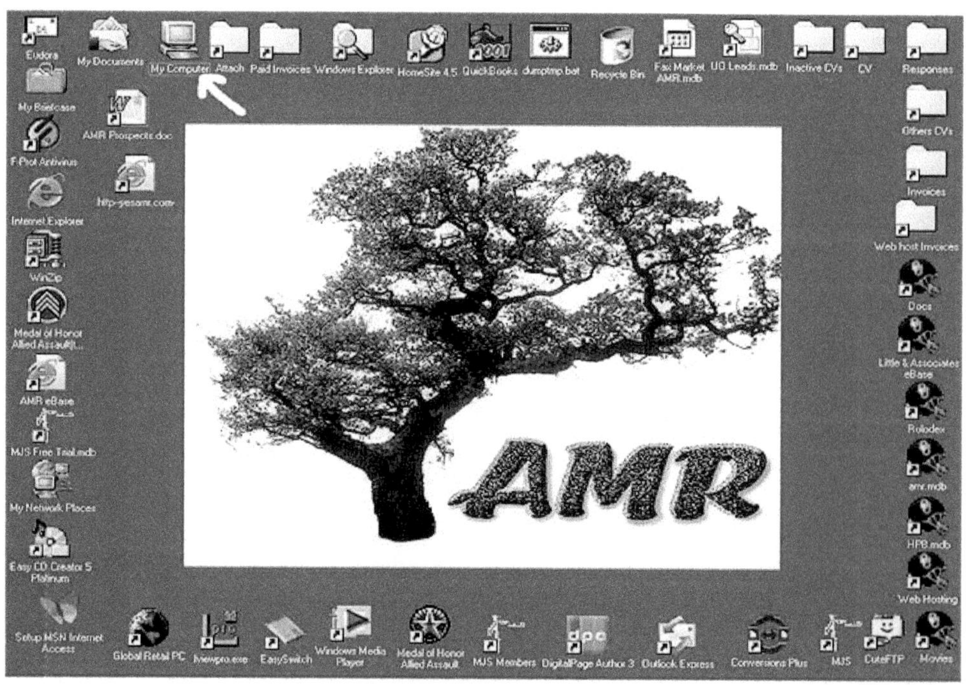

2) You will see your "C" drive. It will say "Local Disk (C:). Double-click on this.

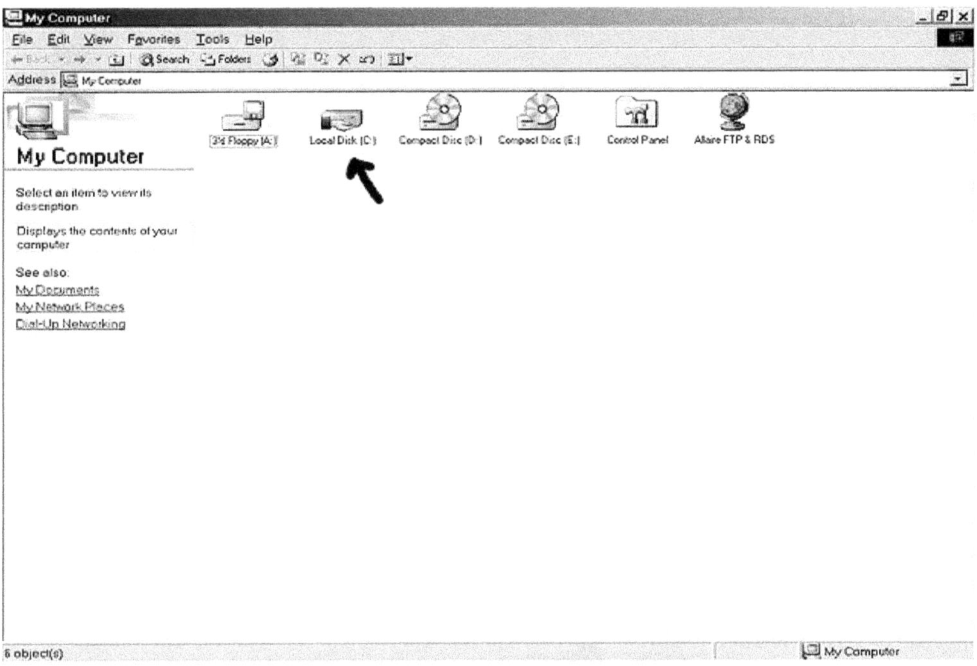

3) After this opens, you will see the folders on your computer.

4) Click "File" from the menu at the top

5) Then, "New" and "Folder".

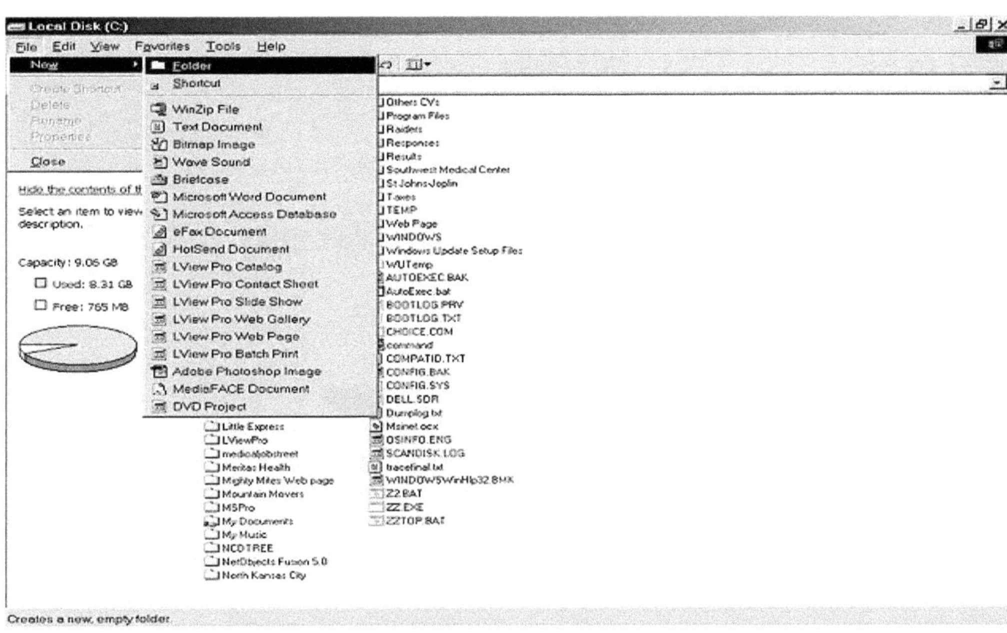

6) You will see a new folder appear below with a blinking cursor beside it that says "New Folder".

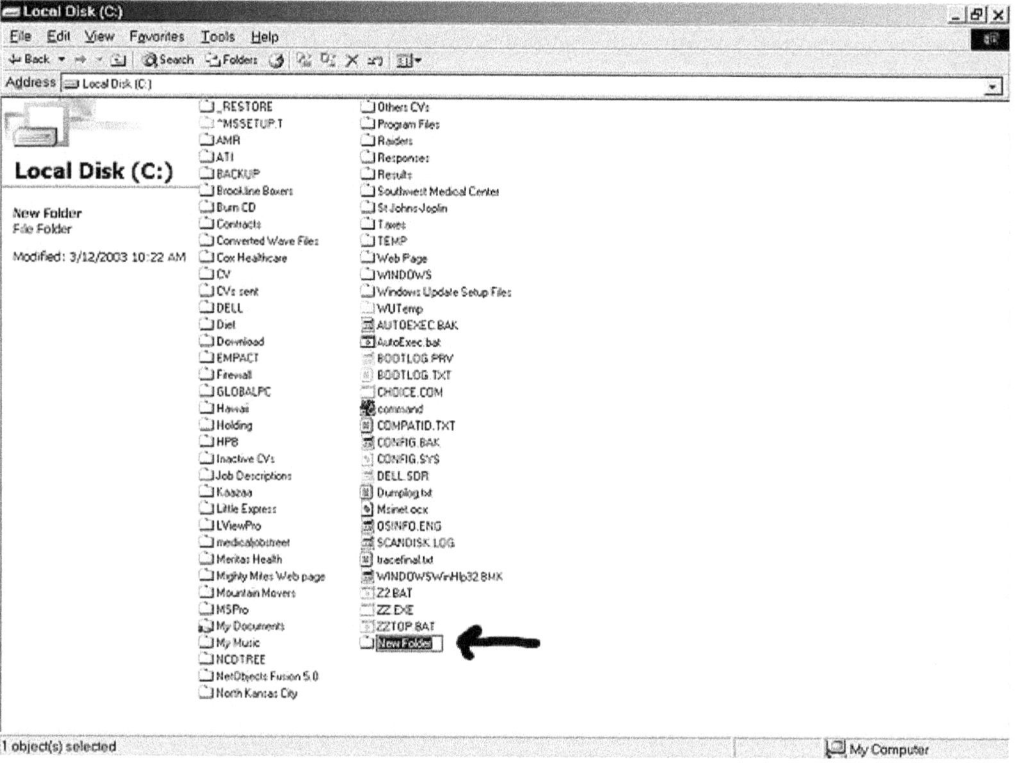

7) Click your mouse cursor inside the part that says "New Folder" and replace that text with whatever you want to name your new folder. It can be more than one word as I described above.

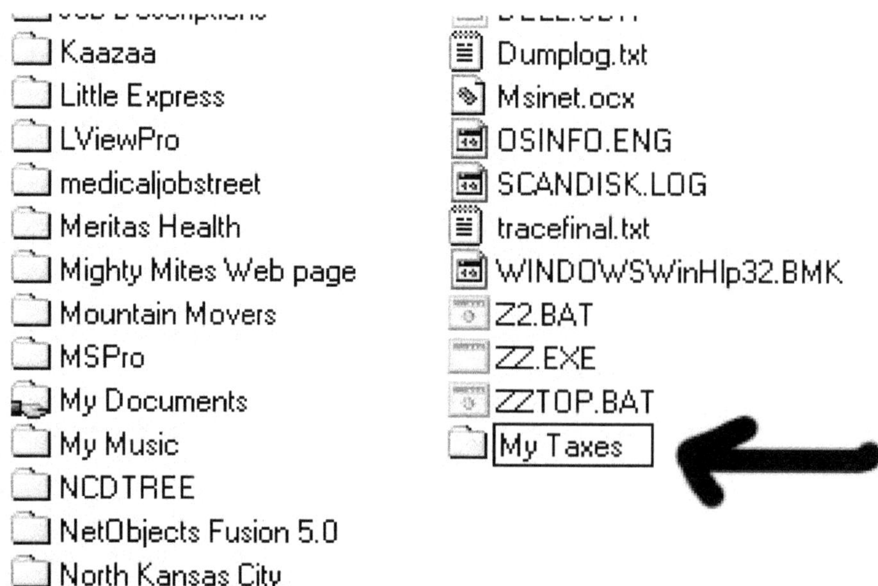

8) Repeat this procedure until you have all the new folders that you will need. You will routinely add new folders as you need them.

Plan to make daily back-ups on every important folder. The most convenient means is a flash drive. These nifty little devices just plug into a USB port on your computer and will store 2, 4 or even 8 Gigs of information.

LESSON TWO: ELECTRONIC DOCUMENTATION METHODS

There are three basic methods to receive documents and we will review all three of these methods:

1) Internal Fax
2) Fax Service
3) Email

INTERNAL FAX

A good, internal fax program is Winfax Pro by Symantacs. There are probably other good programs also, so it is up to you which is the desired fax program. You must, of course, have an independent phone line hooked up to your computer and make sure it is not busy a good deal of the time if you use that same line for your internet connection. If necessary, spend the extra money to have a second phone line for your business and keep one line open to receive faxes.

If you choose to receive faxes with Winfax Pro, make sure you save all faxes in a folder you have created (covered in Lesson One) and is easily accessible. When you "Save as", you can name a document anything you wish. I suggest naming it something that pertains directly to that document or with some type of numerical system pertaining to your particular business.

FAX SERVICE

The second method to receive documents is by a fax/email service. There are many services available. A good example is efax (efax.com).

It is a reasonable cost service and will supply you with a separate number. You may want to sign up for two numbers in case one gets those 'circuits busy'. This does not take a separate phone line running into your office, which is part of the beauty of a fax service. Efax also has an efax plus account which allows you to not only receive, but send a fax . There is an additional transmission time cost when sending a fax.

Efax allows you to indicate the format in which you can receive documents. The best is PDF. This is a universal format and a PDF reader can be downloaded free from adobe.com.

With this service, you can be traveling on a highway, hook your cell phone up to your laptop, get on the internet, and send a fax via efax through your email program. The decision you will have to make is 'how free do you want to be'? It is not free to be free.

EMAIL

The last method of receiving documents (and the best) is by email. We encourage clients to send documents by email attachment or even in the body of the email.

These documents print out like originals and cannot be beat for clarity. Once again, make sure you save all documents in the proper folder you have created.

A word here about email software. I use Eudora Pro, which allows me to easily get attachments; create 'stationary' for repetitive emails; etc. Microsoft Outlook is probably the most popular. Make sure you are signed up with a server which allows you to receive attachments.

Receiving paper documents: If you receive a paper document by mail, simply scan it and save it in one of your electronic folders, as previously covered. Most printers sold now are multi-purpose (fax, print, scan, etc.)

LESSON THREE: SENDING AND RECEIVING DOCUMENTS WITH FAX PROGRAM

Here we will focus on sending and receiving documents electronically by WinFax Pro or other internal fax programs. There are other programs you may want to use, but you will follow similar steps.

WinFax Pro is an internal fax program that works within your computer. To become paperless, you must be able to receive all documents electronically. WinFax is one of those ways.

Remember, you must keep your computer on 24 hours if you don't want to miss any faxes. You may wish to turn off your monitor and printer at night. Make sure the WinFax icon appears in the lower right-hand corner of your Windows start-up screen. WinFax will run in the background at all times. When you install WinFax, make sure you answer “yes” to whether or not you want it on your Windows start-up.

From the WinFax program, click on the menu item "Receive" and click "Automatic receive". Winfax will automatically answer any call coming in to your computer phone line.

When you receive a document, click "Receive Log" to see the document. Double-click the entry of the document to open. It will appear as a one-line entry before clicking.

Now is the time for “Clean Up”. If the document has any kind of logo stamp, fax stamps, etc. that you want to remove, here's where "Annotation" comes in handy. If annotation is open, you should see an “eraser” icon! This is the perfect way to get rid of all the “chicken tracks” and logos on the document. Just click on the eraser and scrub the document clean.

Now you are ready to put your logo or other identification on it if desired. Make sure you have a good system in place to know from where the document originates if needed.

To stamp the document with your logo, click on the stamp icon, then click "New". Find your logo stored (.bmp format) on your hard drive and make sure you type in the description in the "Description" box. This will be the name of your logo on the stamp drop-down list. Now when you click on the stamp icon, your logo will be in the drop-down list of stamps.

Now it is time to save the document. With the document still up, you can save it any one of three ways.

1. You can click on "File", then "Save as". Select a format (fxr is a WinFax format that only Winfax can read, or -pcx, which is an image format that almost any computer

can read). I suggest printing the document, using a PDF program as your printer. This is explained in the third method below. Name it anything you wish and find the proper folder on your hard drive in which to save it. Saving in .fxr is okay if you are always going to fax and not send as an email attachment.

2. The second way to save is by clicking on "File", then "Export". You have a few more format choices here in which to save: tiff, .bmp, .pcx and .dcx are image formats, as well as the .fxr format. Once again, export to the proper folder.

3. The third way (and best way) to save a document is by clicking "File", then "Print". Here you have the option of saving in PDF format.

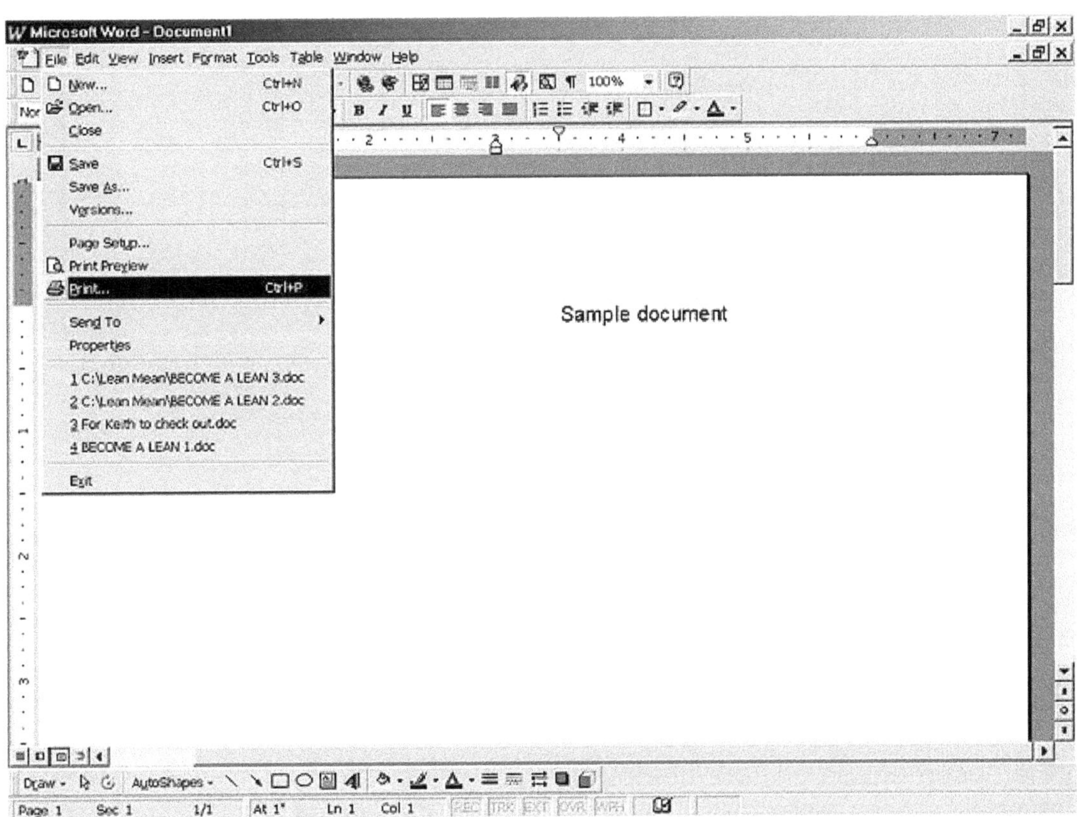

Select your PDF program (like Adobe) as your printer instead of your printer, since both Adobe and WinFax Pro (if you use this internal system) installs themselves as printers. After selecting Adobe as the printer, click “File”, then "Print" and the print menu will pop up.

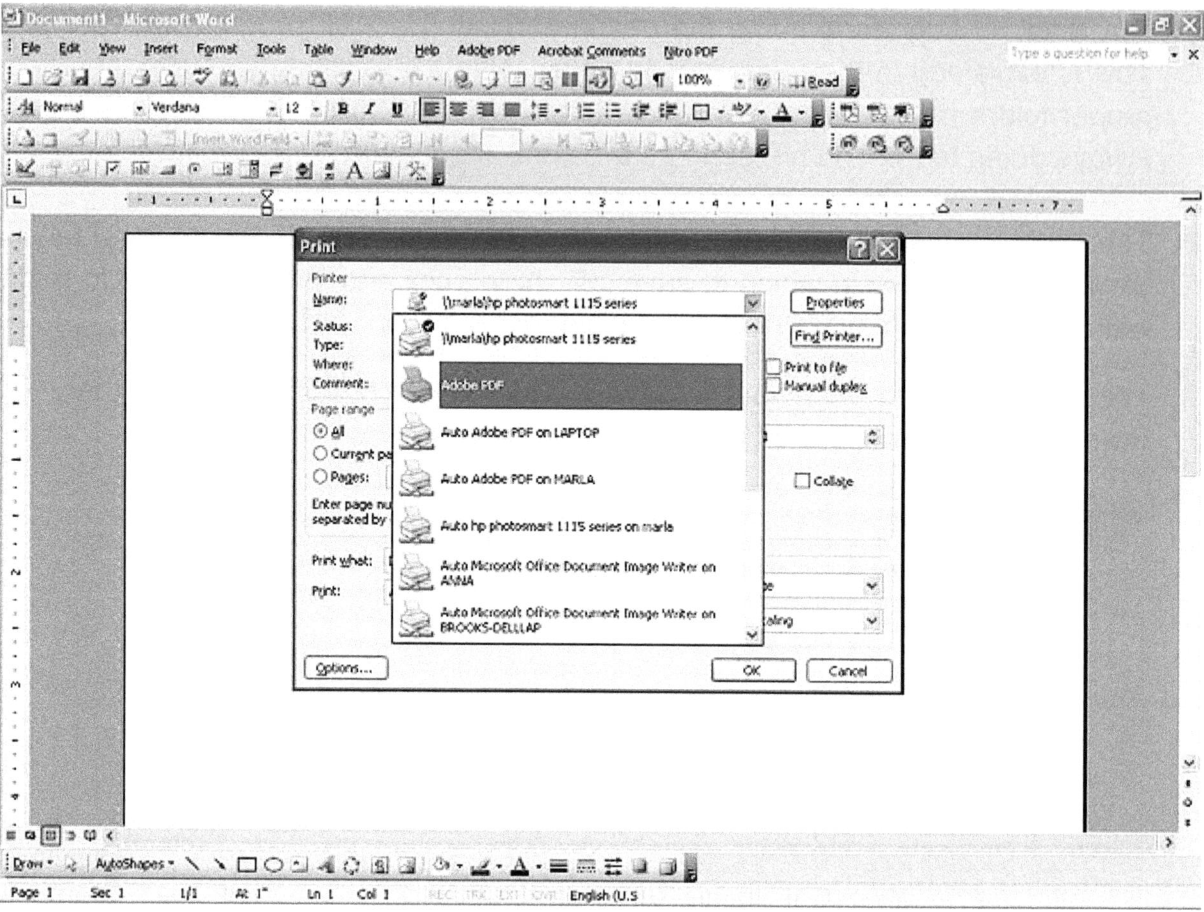

You have three tabs shown on this pop up. "Fax , "Email" and "Save".

Select “Adobe PDF” and it will ask you what to name the document and where you would like it saved.

To send a document with WinFax Pro, you follow these steps:

1. *Bring the document up on your computer
2. *Click "File"
3. *Click "Print"
4. *Select "WinFax Pro" as your printer.
5. *Click "Print" and WinFax will open, ready to send that document with a cover page.

You may also send more than one document from different folders with WinFax Pro.

LESSON FOUR: SENDING AND RECEIVING DOCUMENTS WITH FAX SERVICE

This section focuses on fax services to transfer documents electronically. You need to sign up with a fax service such as efax provided by efax.com. It is a paperless method of receiving and sending faxes by email. Be sure to read the information and regulations on the efax website as policies and cost may change over time.

In the past when a customer signed up with efax, a fax number would be assigned to that customer with no charge. There may now be a small monthly fee for this service. The freedom and convenience is worth it. How free do you want to be?

If you sign up at efax.com and get a free fax number, you can receive faxes through your email address, but currently you cannot send faxes through your email address. The sending of faxes has a small monthly fee plus a few cents per 30 second transmission cost. This minimal cost is worth it to have the freedom to be physically away from the office and still send a fax if necessary. That is done by the use of a cell phone and laptop, notebook or other mobile electronic equipment which contains the material to be faxed.

To receive and/or send a document by efax, first sign up. It's easy. Just go to efax.com and fill out the information on your business. You will be assigned a fax number that is probably not in your area code.

You will be given a choice of area codes, and there may be a local number for your area. But, don't worry about having a fax number with an area code that is different than your phone number. We tell clients that we subscribe to a fax service which gives us clean and clear fax copies. They definitely understand that.

Next, when you set up how you wish to receive documents, indicate you wish them to be sent in PDF format.

Now all you have to do is give your efax number to clients, associates and candidates. When they fax a document to you, it will come to you in your email as an attachment. You simply click on the attachment and your PDF viewer will open the document.

Now that you have the document, what do you *do* with it? If it is an important document, of course, you will want to save it (covered in an earlier lesson of this series). But WAIT; what if you want to put your company logo on it first?

You will need to add your logo to the PDF stamp catalog first. Just follow the instructions within your PDF program for adding a stamp.

To save or export a document, first, delete unwanted pages. This is also explained within your PDF program. Then, from the "File" menu, click "Save as" and name the document anything you wish. Save in PDF format. Find your folder that you created to save this document and save.

SENDING A DOCUMENT WITH EFAX

If you are savvy with sending email attachments, this should be a breeze.

- Go to your email program and prepare an email to whomever.
- Find your attachment button on your email program and find the file you wish to send.
- It's difficult to go through instructions for this since everyone uses different email programs.

If you send a document using the email attachment method, you can send a PDF document.

FAXING WITH EFAX

Simply open your email program as above, select the document as an attachment, then in the "To:" area, instead of an email address, you will type in the following example: 15552223333@efaxsend.com. You must be a paid subscriber of efax to do this.

This doesn't cover everything efax will do (that would take a handbook), but it will get you started on sending and receiving documents by efax.

LESSON FIVE: ELECTRONIC SIGNATURES

In order to be an effective paperless machine, you must have the capability of inserting electronic signatures on documents.

More than likely, most of your clients and customers have an email address. Sending them paperless contracts, documents, or other materials for electronic signature is a snap. Not long ago, laws were passed that made electronic signatures legal. While you won't see this exercised by many right away, it will be the wave of the future. Why not ride it now and impress your clients?

We contract with our clients to perform certain duties. We have the contract on our computer's hard drive and it can simply be copied and pasted in the body of an email to a client. While this particular contract is composed as a contingency agreement with a healthcare entity, the basic idea works with any document needing signature. We use Eudora Pro email software and have our document as "stationery."

We include something along these lines: "Please review the below document and click "Reply" on your Email program. Follow the instructions. Below is an example:

Read all of the terms and conditions of the contingency agreement and If you are in complete agreement, type the following information in the spaces provided below at the bottom of the agreement:

(a) company name,
(b) name of authorized signer and
(c) title of authorized signer

BY USING THE E-SIGNATURE PROCESS DESCRIBED ABOVE YOU AGREE TO ABIDE BY THE CONTINGENCY AGREEMENT BELOW: You would include your agreement below this line.

When we receive the 'signed' contract back, do the following:

- *Click on "File" on our email program
- *And "Save as"
- *Name the document the client's name
- *And save it to our folder "Contracts". We save it in .txt format, which is simple text.

Of course, if your client is not email savvy, you can still receive a signed, paperless document from them.

- Bring up your document which is now located on your hard drive
- Fill in all the required spaces
- Click "File" on your menu.
- Click "Print" and select "WinFax Pro" as your printer.
- Click "OK" and WinFax will open, ready to send the document with a cover page.

Now, depending upon whether you opted to receive faxed documents by WinFax or efax, you will receive the signed contract back paperless. Then, you just save it to the appropriate folder.

LESSON SIX: HARDWARE REQUIREMENTS

Now we come to the part that makes the Lean, Mean Paperless Machine run. You can have the most beautiful car in the world, but it won't run on double A batteries. If you are truly serious about becoming paperless, you must work with serious equipment.

A Pentium computer, with sufficient up-to-date speed and memory would be a starter. I use a Dell laptop, with a speed of 2 Gigahertz with 1 Gig of RAM and sometimes I wish for more. New, faster equipment is coming out all the time, so there are lots of faster machines out there.

The point is; if you try to work at a high speed and need to keep several programs open at the same time with under-powered equipment, you'll experience frustration. You must be willing to invest in the hardware that will do the job.

Part of your equipment will be a scanner. In the real world, you will occasionally receive a document by regular snail mail. Scanner prices are pretty reasonable and there are numerous scanner models from which to choose. You really don't need to spend a lot of money on a scanner that is heralded as a high resolution scanner for pictures

If you want to go another step beyond paperless, consider going wireless. We are now going paperless and wireless (as much as technology allows), but this is still pretty much cutting-edge technology.

Broadband, high-speed wireless connections are now available. Satellite telephones are still a little pricey, but are coming down in price.

The key to this is to have the best available equipment and use it effectively.

LESSON SEVEN: INTERNET DATABASES

Now that we have gone paperless, it is time to consider going the next step; **MOBILE.**

We developed a server based database that lets us do just that. By residing on a server, we may access our database from anywhere we can access the internet. We have been using this database as our internal database since its inception two years ago and we will continue to improve it.

Our internet database is automatically backed up each night. Additionally, we have an email function that allows us to send a backup copy of the data to as an attachment to our own email address. Reason? We have our entire database backed up in two separate locations. Our server also has an eight hour battery back-up in case of power outages. Not only does our internet based database give us the freedom of mobility, but it's a real time-saver.

While there are a number of internet based databases on the market now (just type in "Internet based database" on any internet search engine), you may want a custom database written for your specific needs. It may surprise you how reasonably some programmers price this task. Of course, the price will be higher as you add features. Our internet based database was written by a crackerjack programmer for about $2,000. It is pretty complex and a simple rolodex-style database would be less expensive. Do-it-yourself programs are available that utilize programs like Microsoft Access. The programs simply make access work on a web site.

Basically, though, one advantage of having a paperless office is that it can also be a very mobile office.

With a laptop, notebook, PDA, cell phone, etc. you can run your business wherever you have reception and electricity. It is just that simple. What is stopping you?

Section Four:

Resources, Biographies, & Testimonials

RESOURCES

Recruiting

Alliance of Medical Recruiters	www.allianceofmedicalrecruiters.com
Medical Job Street	www.medicaljobstreet.com
Salary Surveys	www.alliedphysicians.com/salary-surveys

Candidate & Specialty Research

Administrators in Medicine: Licensure verification	www.docboard.org/aim
American Academy of Physician Assistants	saaapa.aapa.org
American Board of Medical Specialties	www.abms.org
American Medical Association	www.ama-assn.org
American Osteopathic Association	www.osteopathic.org
Association of American Medical Colleges: Specialty Pages	www.aamc.org/students/cim/specialties.htm
Bureau of Labor and Statistics: Physicians & Surgeons	www.bls.gov/oco/ocos074.htm
Canadian Medical Association	www.cma.ca
Choice Trust: Physician research	www.choicetrust.com
Federation of State Medical Boards: Directory	www.fsmb.org/directory_smb.html
Physician Reports: Physician Research	www.physicianreports.com
Quack Watch: Health Fraud Research	www.quackwatch.com

Medical Research & Industry News

Medical Group Management Association: Industry news	www.mgma.com
Merck Manuals: Online Medical Library	www.merck.com/mmpe/index.html
Reuters Health: Health & Medical News	www.reutershealth.com/en/index.html
The National Library of Medicine	www.nlm.nih.gov

Legal

Lawyers.com: Find lawyers by state	www.lawyers.com
Robert Lubin & Associates: Immigration Specialist	www.rlapc.com
State malpractice law summaries	www.mcandl.com/states.html
U.S. Equal Employment Opportunity Commission	www.eeoc.gov

Business Resources

AddMe: Add your web page to search engines	www.addme.com
EFax: Online Fax Service	www.efax.com
House Call: Free Online Virus Scan	housecall.trendmicro.com
Score: Business Advice and information	www.score.org
Linked In: Connect with other professionals	www.linkedin.com

Relocation

Economic Research Institute: Salary and Cost of Living information	www.erieri.com
Great Schools: School research	www.greatschools.org
Move: Relocation research and information	www.move.com
Salary Calculator	www.bestplaces.net/col
City Data: Find data on any US City	www.city-data.com

Additional Related Resources

Address.com: Look up numbers and addresses	www.addresses.com
AnyWho: At&t free directory	www.anywho.com
Creative Mailers: Marketing products	www.creativemailers.net
State Abbreviations	www.stateabbreviations.us
Switchboard	www.switchboard.com
United States Postal Service: Zip Code Lookup	zip4.usps.com/zip4/citytown_zip.jsp
US Census	www.census.gov
US Census: American Fact Finder	factfinder.census.gov
US Time Zones	www.time.gov
White Pages: Area Code Lookup	www.whitepages.com/area-codes
Wikipedia: Free Encyclopedia	www.wikipedia.org

BIOGRAPHIES: ABOUT THE AUTHORS

Angela Allen-Cornelius attended Southwest Missouri State University in Springfield, Missouri where she received a Bachelor's Degree in Psychology. Angela had a special interest in behavioral psychology as well as learning theory. She worked for 12 years in social services programs working directly with individuals with autism and youth in the foster care system. She eventually pursued staff development, training, and education within these programs. She wrote and developed the educational curriculum for two agencies and instructed most of the courses. She left to pursue a career that would allow her more flexibility and independence. She started the Allen Cornelius Group, a medical recruitment and consulting firm. In 2007, Angela finished her Master's of Business Administration. She combined her success in training, recruitment experience, and business education to co-develop "The Recruiter Guide". She feels this information is critical for an individual looking for a successful career in medical recruiting. Angela is married and spends her days catering to the needs of her two Siberian Huskies and a Labrador.

Marla Little received her Bachelor's Degree from Truman University in Kirksville, Missouri. After doing some graduate work, she taught English in the public school system. A move to Springfield, Missouri, paved a new career in the Public Relations, grant writing arena for non profits. Her marriage to Randy Little opened a new career area in which she has excelled for 20 years, the healthcare recruitment arena. In 1995, she and her husband Randy began The Alliance of Medical Recruiters, a large network of independent healthcare recruitment firms. After 20 years of successful recruitment; training of new recruits; and daily operation of a successful network, Marla put her knowledge and expertise to work co-developing this comprehensive healthcare recruitment manual. In her words, "If you want a successful career in physician recruitment, you don't have to look any further than this guide." Marla is cofounder of Little & Associates, Inc., a healthcare recruitment company. She is married to Randy Little and they share their home with their three boxers.

Randy T. Little attended the University of Oklahoma where he played football for the Sooners. After an injury, he completed his degree in Computer Science and Accounting at Phillips University (now known as Western Oklahoma University) in Enid, Oklahoma. He began a successful regional sales career in sporting goods and owned and operated a retail sporting goods and taxidermy shop. Following his marriage to Marla Little, he began his career in healthcare recruitment. In 1995 at the urging of healthcare recruiters, Randy developed The Alliance of Medical Recruiters, the longest running network of independent healthcare recruiters. In addition to the daily operations of AMR as well as MedicalJobStreet.com, Randy develops and hosts web sites. Randy is cofounder of Little & Associates, Inc., a healthcare recruitment company. He is married to Marla Little and they share their home with their three boxers.

TESTIMONIALS

"The Recruiter Guide" is a must have for anyone considering becoming a recruiter! From the ground floor up, this guide will give you the basic knowledge on starting your recruiting business the right way, eliminating the frustrations of who, want, when, and where on your own. Very glad these recruiters published what they so graciously shared with me as I started my recruiting business.

Rebecca Woods,
Woods Medical Recruiting

What a gift "The Recruiter Guide" is to new physician recruiters! This excellent manual provides a good orientation to the field of physician recruiting and gives lots of tips and strategies that will make training much easier. Experienced recruiters will benefit from the simple forms and formats provided and will appreciate the systematic approach to organizing the day. A step by step plan for providing good service and making money is offered. A glossary of reference terms and many resource sources are included. This manual provides all the information that is needed to get started or to streamline your work. The book is a must have in any recruiter's library.

Susan Craig
President
Susan Craig Associates Inc.

www.ingramcontent.com/pod-product-compliance
Ingram Content Group UK Ltd.
Pitfield, Milton Keynes, MK11 3LW, UK
UKHW051137260726
13967UKWH00010B/3113